NEW YOU

Discovering the way to . . .
NEW power and peace!

John F. DeVries

THE
NEW YOU

A six-week devotional guide through which You will discover NEW power and peace by looking at yourself in the light of Christ who dwells in you.

Dr. John De Vries is founder of a Christian non-profit organization called Mission India. You will notice frequent references to the people of India in this book. You will also sense his deep love for India and his intense desire to see this nation transformed through the new sense of personal value Christ brings when He inhabits us. John invites you to visit the Mission India website at www. Missionindia.org. Or you may contact Mission India at (877) 644-6342 or email at info@missionindia.org if you would like to learn more about Mission India.

Contents

Acknowledgments

I gratefully acknowledge the tremendous input of my wife, Adelaide, who has provided suggestions and counsel for every meditation in this book.

I also want to express deep appreciation to the "editorial committee," probably the most unique one in the world, consisting of Ken and Lois Blake, Ray Buckner, and Vincent Field.

Week One

"Where Are You, Jesus?"

"Arise, shine, for your light has come, and the
glory of the Lord has risen upon you . . . . And
nations [people] will come to your light."
Isaiah 60:1, 4

Day One: Introduction
"Just who do you think you are?"

Some time ago I was passing a car which was
speeding when I noticed a police officer pulling
over the car. I thought it best that I also stop.
The police officer walked up to my car and said,
"Pulling over was a very wise move." I politely
agreed with him and gave him my license and
registration. He told me he would take care of
me after he wrote up the other driver.

Instead of approaching the driver's side of my
car upon his return, he opened the passenger's
side and got in. Shutting the door he turned to
me and said, "And now, Rev. DeVries, how do
you feel about women's ordination in the

church?" It turned out that he had a double identity. Not only was he a police officer but he was also an elder in our denomination, in which the issue of women's ordination was a very hot topic of discussion at that moment. Suddenly I had an unusual conversation on my hands that had not only theological but also economic implications!

Had the man come to my car dressed in casual clothes I might well have asked him, "Just who do you think you are?" But since he came with his badge and uniform, driving a police cruiser, I did not ask his identity. It was obvious. He knew who he was and why he was stopping me and I also recognized him as being a police officer.

Christians have a "double identity." I did not understand that during the early years. Whenever I looked inside myself all I saw was failure. I was depressed, even though I was a Christian. I did not know who I was because I never thought of Christ as the One Who dwelt in me. He was always a light outside of me, shining down on me. In spite of the fact that His presence in the believer is mentioned over 160 times in the New Testament I refused to look beyond my failure and sin. I did not know who I was in Christ and hence was not tapping into the divine power Christ reserved for me.

The answer to the question "Just who do you think you are?" is not the same for many Christians as the answer to a similar question, "Who are you?" God's answer to our true identity (and Satan's answer) often is radically different than who we think we are. Christians many times build their identity and value in the same way non-Christians do. They base it on possessions and accomplishments. They are often discouraged and depressed, looking at their sins and failures. They fail to see the infinite, unlimited power available to them through the indwelling presence of Christ. They do not grasp Peter's amazing statement that we are "participants in the divine nature" (2 Peter 1:4) and as such share in God's authority over "principalities and powers" (Ephesians 6:12, Luke 9:1). They do not realize that they are God's "closest relatives" (Genesis 1:27) and are higher than the angels who were created as ministering servants. They often fail to grasp that the light of Christ is not shining down on them but is in them shining out and that light drives out demonic darkness. They forget that they are rivers of eternal life, whose effects keep multiplying supernaturally (Ezekiel 47:1-12, John 7:38 and Ephesians 3:20). They do not rejoice in the fact that they are the residences of the King of Kings and Lord of Lords (1 Corinthians 3:16). They do not understand that they are God's police force, charged with authority over the demonic world such as Christ gave to His disciples (Luke 9:1). They do not thrill in their "armor of light" (Romans 13:12) and until they understand that they have been given the uniform and badge of prayer, which makes the demons tremble at the sight of the divine light flowing from them, they will continue to work in fallible, weak human power. But once they put on the uniform of prayer and live as Christ's police force, they will experience an awesome, transforming power.

There is another reason for this book. The poor are often locked in a perpetual, generational lack of personal value, resulting in a bad self-image. Often this bad self-image robs them of vision, courage, and the ability to tackle the many obstacles they face. Instead of presenting salvation merely as some "future ticket" from hell to heaven, salvation must be presented as the divine power to heal them inwardly *at this moment*. They must learn that through the indwelling presence of Christ, they share in Christ's infinite value and purpose.

The "editorial committee" that helped shape this course was made up of two, transformed African American ex-convicts and a white woman who was horribly abused as a child. I drew heavily upon their advice, shaping this material to reach the broken people to whom they now minister. They feel that the core problem of some poor is the lack of motivation to change, which is the direct result of low self-esteem and personal worth. Motivation is like gas to a car; the best car doesn't go far without fuel. Christ in us is the source of infinite value and unlimited power and resources and hence becomes the motivational power, the spiritual fuel, which drives transformation. The identity God gives us by Christ's presence in us, our new identity, is the source of courage, vision, and confidence. The devil knows who we are and wants to keep that a secret from us. If he can just lead us to concentrate on our sins and failures and ignore what Christ has made us to be, he knows he will never be "arrested." We pray that both those who call themselves Christians and those seeking to understand what following Christ means will be transformed through this book.

The format:
Meaningful knowledge consists of three activities: learn it, do it, and share it. Doing these three activities ensures growth in real, practical knowledge. These activities are built into each of the devotionals.

The "learn it" experience consists of:
- A memory verse for each week, divided into five daily thoughts.
- Five daily devotionals that explain each thought. The phrase of the verse for the day is printed in italics.
- A set of discussion questions at the end of each devotional.

The **"do it" experience consists of** solving a practical life problem by using the teaching of each devotional.

The **"share it" experience occurs** during the discussions of the "Learn it" and "Do it" questions at the end of each devotional.

The course is primarily designed for family or private devotions. It also is an excellent six-week small-group study. It is also an excellent test book for home schools. The daily devotions can be read privately. Group discussion follows daily or weekly by sharing answers to the "Learn it" and "Do it" questions at the end of each devotional.

* * * * *

Day Two: "Wake up to who you are in Christ!"

"Arise . . ." Isaiah 60:1

I was born twenty-five pounds overweight, a condition from which I have yet to recover! Well, obviously the first part isn't true, but if you'd see me you'd know that the second part of that sentence is no exaggeration. Because I've always been overweight, I gained the nickname "fat stuff" early in life. And that nickname, combined with a total lack of coordination and athletic ability, didn't do much for creating a good self-image.

Consequently I went through life suffering much depression caused by a sense of failure. I was always chosen last for a ball team because I would insure that the side that chose me would be defeated. As I grew older I found that my bad self-image and sense of worthlessness made me very depressed at times.

I'm sharing this, not because I'm so unusual but rather because everyone suffers to a greater or lesser degree from feelings of failure and worthlessness. None of us seem to be satisfied with our looks; our ears are too big or our nose is too long or we are too tall or too short. We never have enough money or possessions. We never are satisfied!

Worldwide, people have very serious problems with feelings of worthlessness. The caste system in India teaches that there are people who are worthless or outcaste. Some people may have been abused emotionally or sexually by parents, relatives, or friends, with resulting feelings of worthlessness, poor self-image, and lack of purpose. One of the reasons for alcoholism and drug abuse is failure to be able to look at ourselves. We need an escape and find it in drugs and alcohol. Feelings of lack of significance, poor self-image, and no purpose in life are far more common than we realize. They exist in every country, among all people.

My life has been spent in founding and developing Mission India. I remember an Indian pastor crying during a prayer time with a team of American pastors I had taken there. When the prayer was over he apologized, saying that as we prayed he had been attacked by Satan. He had been an "untouchable" and the devil accused him of pride. "How can you, an untouchable, place yourself on a level with these Americans?" the devil taunted. "You have no right to be praying with Americans! You are an untouchable!" Then suddenly the Holy Spirit reminded him of who he REALLY was, namely, a child of the King who had royal blood spilled over him. He received a new sense of self-worth and dignity. His self-image and his purpose in life were restored because of Christ Who lived in him.

We all long to step out of the shadows into the light, but we don't really know how. We keep looking at ourselves, trying to overcome our failures and improve our appearance, but it doesn't work. No matter how much fame or money or power we get, these things only temporarily, at best, help us in feeling positive about ourselves.

There is another way to build a good self-image and gain a satisfying sense of value. That's what this book is all about. Being born again is not merely getting a "ticket" that saves you from going to hell after you die and gets you into heaven. Yes, people who are born again won't go to hell, but that's not the real meaning of being born again. Being born again isn't some magical **ticket** but it is an inner **transformation**. The Bible says it is being made new. "If anyone is in **Christ he is a new creation,** the old has gone and the new has come" (2 Corinthians 5:17). Being born again means that we are "in Christ." This little devotional is intended to help us build a new self-image by looking at the One Who lives in us rather than by looking at our physical attractiveness, or our money, or what others say about us. When we discover the One in us, when we find His importance, His power, His beauty, His light and life, then we will have not only a NEW sense of value and a NEW self-image, but we'll also have a NEW sense of purpose and meaning in life. We will go from gloom to joy!

Learn it:

1. How does the first illustration picture the way many people feel, and how does the second express what we would like to have happen to us?
2. What are some of the things that happen to people which destroy their sense of value?
3. When do people feel they have no purpose in life?
4. What are some of the most common ways in which most people try to establish a sense of personal value? Why don't these work?

Do it:

Ken grew up believing that if only he got an education everything would be alright. He pursued getting two doctoral degrees and was nearly successful when his closest loved one was tragically killed. Everything fell apart and Ken sank into deep despair, feeling that life was worthless. Do you know of people in similar situations and how do we normally comfort them? How would you counsel Ken based on this devotion?

Prayer: Lord, may we step out of the gloom into Your light today. For Your sake, Jesus, Amen.

* * * * *

Day Three: "Understanding the functions of light."

"Arise, *Shine* . . ." Isaiah 60:1

When I found this picture, I fell in love with it. I've shared it with many people since who have had the same reaction to it. When I ask, "What do you like about this picture?" the answer is always the same. They like the light. And I pursue the question by asking, "What do you like about the light?" Answers range from liking the glow, the warmth, and the inviting nature of the light to the fact that the light invites them to the house. If they were out walking they would not hesitate to go up to this house, but if there were no lights on they would be a little fearful. The light invites us, it attracts us.

Light has many functions. Among its many functions I would list these:

- **Light destroys darkness**. A little fellow, a hundred years ago, was watching a lamp lighter come down the street when his mom asked what he was doing. He replied that he was watching a man punch holes in the darkness. Darkness cannot withstand light.
- **Light shows the path**. The light from this house shows the way to the house. Whenever there is light we can see the way, the path. Jesus, as the light of the world, shatters the darkness and illuminates the way to the Father.
- **Light shows beauty**. Any photographer or artist knows the importance of light in a photograph or painting. Light, carefully applied, makes a picture come to life.
- **Light lifts emotions**. In the area in which I live one winter we had forty-four consecutive days of rain and thirteen days in which there was no sunshine at all. Folks living around here appreciate a sunny day more than others and emotions soar when the sun finally shines.
- **Light gives life**. Finally, light and life are inseparably linked together. House flowers lean toward the light. Hot houses that are lighted 24/7 grow tremendous plants. Light gives life.

As we look at this house there is something more to light. It is a symbol of two important things; it is a symbol of life and of love. The house is occupied and seems warm and inviting because it is a symbol of love. A family must live here, a loving family.

This picture has helped me imagine what I must look like since I am born again. To be born again means that "I was crucified with Christ and I no longer live but Christ lives in me" (Galatians 2:20). I remember well the first time this truth dawned on me. I was reading Psalm 27:1, "The Lord is my light . . ." I could not get beyond that phrase and a question kept popping up in my mind. "Where is the light, John? Where is the light?" I kept answering, saying, "The light is out there, shining down on me." Finally, I realized that the light was in me, shining out of me. And when I saw that I thought, "I must stop kicking myself around. The 'light of the world' is in me and that gives me tremendous value!" My value doesn't come from my appearance any more than that house in the picture is attractive because of its architecture. It's the light . . . the light shining from within me . . . that's what matters.

Suddenly God gave me a tool to begin to rebuild that lousy self-image, that self-centered drive for perfectionism. Fat stuff died! He was crucified with Christ and all my sins were paid for. I gained a totally new way of looking at myself. And that's what I want to share with you through these devotionals with the hope that you will discover the "new you," the transformation that being born again brings right now.

Learn it:
1. What do you like about the picture of the house?
2. What are five functions of light?
3. What are the two symbols of light as shown in this picture?
4. How is this a picture of 2 Corinthians 5:17?

Do it:
Ken thought education would satisfy but found that it could not fill the void left by the murder of his loved one. You are called to counsel him. The picture of the house is the picture of what you look like spiritually. How does this picture of the house give us encouragement to help others?

Prayer: Savior, help us to look at ourselves not in terms of our works, or deeds, or physical attractiveness or lack of it. Holy Spirit, help us to look at ourselves in terms of Christ in us, the hope of glory. For Your sake, Jesus, Amen.

* * * * *

Day Four: "The Light is IN you!"

"Arise, shine, *for your light
has come* . . ." Isaiah 60:1

One of the most famous and well-loved verses of
the Bible is John 3:16. *"For God so loved the world
He gave His one and only Son that whoever believes
in Him should not perish but have eternal life."*
What is this "eternal life" that Jesus speaks about?
Is it something that happens only when our bodies die? Or is eternal life something which starts
now? We must be able to answer this question in
order to build a new sense of value and a new
self-image on the basis of Christ in us, rather than
on what we look like or what we have done. Most
of us think of eternal life as something which
starts after death.

The Bible teaches us that eternal life starts now.
It is placed in us when we believe in Christ. This

is the implication that Paul gives when he describes himself in these words: "I was crucified with Christ and I no longer live but Christ lives in me" (Galatians 2:20). He doesn't speak in a future tense. He doesn't say, "When I die I will then live for ever." Rather he says he has died already. He claims he was crucified with Christ. But what does he mean? What was crucified? Let's call it the old self—the sinful self. The sinful self is the one which exists on the principle of living to get. That controlling principle is dead because we are now filled with Christ. "Fat stuff" doesn't live anymore. He is done. When I discovered that Christ lived in me, I didn't need to have good looks or athletic ability to feel good about myself. I was occupied by the greatest Being in the universe, Jesus Christ. What matters is that Christ lives in me now and that He uses me to reveal Himself to the world. I have a whole new value, a whole new purpose in life.

How does this work? How is Christ in me? Jesus uses the illustration of a vine and a branch found in John 15:1 to help us understand. Just as the vine delivers life to the branch, so our relationship is so close to Christ that His life flows into us. We become new, fruitful, productive, transformed people.

What is this new, eternal life which is delivered to us as a vine delivers life to the branch? This new life is the power to give or produce. It is the power to be selfless. It is the power to consider others before we think of ourselves. Just as the life in the vine enables the branches to produce (and give) fruit, so the life of Christ in us enables us to give good things to others. One of these gifts is giving the light of Jesus to others by doing good things for them.

In John 9:5 Jesus said, "**While I am in the world** *I am the light of the world."* He qualified the statement, *"I am the light of the world."* when He said that He was the light of the world *only as long as He was in the world* in His human nature. Christ is in the world in a totally different way now, than when He lived in Palestine. Christ is in the world by being in His disciples through His Holy Spirit. This allows Him to say of us that "You are the light of the world" (Matthew 5:14). We are the light not in our power but in His power. We are connected to the "Power Source." Just as the house in our picture would have no light without connection to electricity, so we have no light without the connection of faith to Jesus Christ.

Each day, upon arising, we should remind ourselves of three things by praying the "New You Prayer".

1. "Where are You, Jesus?" Jesus says, "I am in you" (Galatians 2:20).
2. "Who are You, Jesus?" Jesus says, "I am the light of the world" (John 9:5).

3. "What do You want, Jesus?" Jesus says, I want you to turn on My light today and let it shine out of you" (Matthew 5:14).

Learn it:
1. What does Jesus' resurrection mean (1 Corinthians 15:35–58)?
2. When does eternal life start (Galatians 2:20)?
3. How does eternal life flow into us (John 15:1–5)?
4. What do you think abiding or remaining in Christ means (John 15:7)?
5. What promise is given to those who remain in Christ (John 15:7)?
6. What is the purpose of remaining in Christ (John 15:8)?

Do it:
How could you use these pictures to help Ken get out of his depression and begin to hope again?

Prayer: Savior, these thoughts are difficult to understand. Help us to think of life flowing through the vine into the branch as we think of our relationship to You. Help us to think of that house being connected to the electricity. May we see that our light has come, and it is in us. Savior, You live in us. For Your sake we pray, Amen.

* * * * *

Day Five: "Let the Light shine out of you."

"Arise, shine, for your light
has come *and the glory of the Lord
will rise upon you.*" Isaiah 60:1

What is the "glory" of the Lord? What is this
beautiful thing that will rise on us and shine out
of us? It is *love;* love expressed in selfless sacrifice.
It is generous love, giving love. It is the love which
the Father has lavished on us (I John 3:1) meaning that He gives so generously it spills out over
everything.

We must never think of the "glory" of the Lord
as being His power, although it certainly is that.
The height of God's beauty is love. God used the
sin in the world as the occasion to show the greatest possible expression of love. "But God demon-

strates His own love for us in this: While we were still sinners, Christ died for us" (Romans 5:8).

Paul says that we all find it hard to give up our life for a good person, but it is virtually unheard of to give up our life for our enemies. But while we were enemies of God, rebelling against Him through our selfishness, God gave the life of His Son for us.

Sin can be described as breaking God's peace or harmony. God created the world to be in perfect harmony or unity with Him and within itself. He created humans to be in perfect unity with Him. Sin is that which destroys that harmony and when that harmony is destroyed, God's creation is destroyed.

Harmony is destroyed by selfish getting; getting without concern for hurting others. When we want power, money, position, or fame and we do not care who gets hurt in our getting it, we are sinning against God first of all, then against our fellow human beings, and finally against God's creation.

I have often told the story of the fruit tree that kept all its fruit stacked in a pyramid around its trunk. I heard it pray, "Thank You, God, for allowing me to keep all my fruit. I cannot believe how blessed I am. Look at all the other trees. They not only don't have any fruit right now, they don't even have any leaves." Then I heard God crying as He said, "My precious fruit tree, what ever made you think I created you to keep your fruit?

I created you to give it away. You have destroyed my purpose for you and even now the maggots are eating the fruit and soon will be entering your trunk to destroy you."

The light that dwells in us and flows from us shows itself in our concern for the sick, the poor, the prisoners, the helpless, and the forgotten ones. This is the "fruit" that God expects us to produce, when Christ lives in us. God's glory is seen not in how high and exalted He is, but in how low He could stoop in His love and concern for us.

The mark of true followers of Jesus is found not in how high they can climb but in how low they can reach down. The beauty of Jesus, which we long to have seen in us, is found in our concern for the fatherless and the widows (James 1:27).

Learn it:

1. For what purpose did Christ come according to Luke 4:16–19?
2. Why was Sodom destroyed (Ezekiel 16: 49–50)? What does that mean for our wealth?
3. What aspects of Christ's glory (beauty) are described in Philippians 2:6–11?
4. What is the value of one lost person according to Matthew 18:10–14?

Do it:

How does helping others, who have experienced tragedy enable us to deal with our own tragedies?

What advice would you give to Ken (Day 1) based on this devotion?

Prayer: Savior, help us to see that the beauty and light that are the most important to You are found in concern for the forgotten and the lost. Grant that we may not seek to climb to the heights but rather may be willing to join You in giving to reach the lowest of the low. May Your light shine through us in this as we are concerned for the hurting and hungry people around us. For Your sake we pray, Amen.

* * * * *

Day Six: "Christ's light shining out of you will attract others to you."

"Arise, shine, for your light has come
and the glory of the Lord is risen upon you . . .
and nations (people) will come to your light."
Isaiah 60:1, 3

We are back where we started, looking at the light
streaming from this house. Remember, it's the
light, not the lines of the house, that attract us.
What is true for this house—that the light from
within it is that which attracts others—is also true
for each disciple of Jesus. It is not our physical
beauty (although we should always be neat) which
attracts others. Sometimes we can dress and adorn
ourselves in such a way that people cannot possi-

bly see through us to Jesus! It is not our position, nor our possessions, nor our success by worldly standards that is to be the basis of our personal value. It's the light of Jesus within us, shining out of us, with all its beckoning warmth.

Remember, there are two requirements for the light to shine. The first one, as you look at this picture of the house, is the fact that the house must be wired and connected to the power supply. When storms come and the power supply is interrupted, the lights go out. We need always to be "connected" to Christ. In John 15 Christ gives us the command that we must "abide" in Him and then He will "abide" in us. Paul explains this in Galatians 2:20 when he says, "The life I live in the body, I live by faith in the Son of God, Who loved me and gave Himself for me." When Paul says he is living by faith, he means that he is living by looking at Jesus and trusting Him, not looking at himself and trying to acquire things for himself. Jesus Christ is our power connection.

But it is not enough to be connected to the power by trusting Jesus. We must turn on the lights, by turning the switch to "on." The "on" position which allows the light of Christ to flow into us and out of us is spelled "GIVE." The off position is spelled "GET." Each time we are self-ish, we turn the light of Christ off. We must "give" ourselves to Christ in the sense that we allow Him to penetrate every part of our being with His spirit of generosity.

A new sense of value comes from seeing the importance of the One living in us. We will look at that next week. And based on His importance we can start to build and experience a new attitude toward ourselves. These two experiences, of value and a positive self-image, will result in a new purpose in life. That new purpose can be summarized in the functions of light.

- Light destroys darkness. Our new mission and purpose in life is to destroy darkness!
- Light shows the way to the Father. This is our new task to tell others about Jesus and thus point all to the Father!
- Light reveals beauty. Our whole purpose is to radiate the generous, loving, beautiful concern of the Father for the smallest in the world.
- Light lifts emotions. The Savior comforts others through our words, our deeds, our love.
- Light brings life. More than all else this is our highest calling. We are life-givers to those who are spiritually dead.

There is no room for us to feel miserable about ourselves if we are born again. Being born again is not a ticket but a transformation from darkness to light!

Learn it:
1. What are the two requirements for the light to shine from this house?
2. How are these also the two requirements for Christ's light to shine from within us?
3. What was Paul's power connection according to the second part of Galatians 2:20?
4. What is the spiritual "off" switch which keeps the light of Christ from flowing out of us?
5. What is the "on" switch?

Do it:
We have a new purpose in life, which is summarized in the functions of light mentioned in this devotional. How would you apply those five functions of light to Ken's (Day 1) situation?

Prayer: Savior, thank You for showing us a new, transformed way of living. Help us to discover the new person You have created in us and to live with our minds fixed on You. In Your name we pray, Amen.

* * * * *

Day Seven: Reflection

1. What did you like about the devotions this week?
2. Was there anything that you did not like or did not understand?
3. What unique new lessons did you learn about God?
4. Did this lesson help you in any practical way? Explain how.

Week Two

"Who Are You, Jesus"

"In the beginning was the Word, and the Word was with God and the Word was God. He was with God in the beginning. Through Him all things were made: without Him nothing was made that has been made. In Him was life, and that life was the light of men."
John 1:1–4

Day One: Introduction

One of the most important offices in the world is the office of the president of the United States. Meeting in this office with his advisors he makes decisions that affect not only the citizens of the United States but people in other nations as well.

Can you imagine visiting this office? Can you imagine sitting in on some of the morning briefings? Can you imagine that the president of the United States would actually invite you to come, perhaps monthly or weekly, to listen to your views and your requests?

How would you feel? Like this?

Of course not! You would feel like this!

Every one of us would have a profound new sense of importance! Our whole self-image would be transformed. Feelings of failure would be gone. We would have a tremendous sense of purpose.

Now imagine something more strange. Imagine that the president did not invite you to his office, but rather invited himself to your house. Imagine that he asked you if he could come to your house and visit you. That's so far-fetched it is difficult to even think of.

But there is Someone knocking on your door. Every day when you get up that Someone knocks. Have you ever wondered Who that Person is? It is Someone far more important than any person on earth. It is Jesus Christ. One of the reasons we don't know "who we are" is because we spend so little time thinking about Who He is! It is easy to understand that we can get a sense of importance from being with the president. Doesn't it make sense that if Someone far more important than the president wants to come into our life and live with us, we should have a totally new self-image? When we say we are Christians but feel like we are failures, we are saying that the One Who lives in us really doesn't matter! It would be like saying that it would not matter if the president or prime minister came to our house.

Just Who is Jesus? How important is He? We will be looking at that subject this week as we review the five descriptions of Jesus which we find in John 1:1-4.

- Christ in us . . . the way to God.
- Christ in us . . . the greatness of God.
- Christ in us . . . the knowledge of God.
- Christ in us . . . the creating God.
- Christ in us . . . the life-giving God.

Learn it:
1. In what way is the president's office one of the most important offices in the world?
2. What would happen to your sense of value, your self-image, and your purpose in life if you were invited to this office each week?
3. Why would being in this office weekly make you feel important?
4. Is there anyone greater and more powerful than the people who fill this office?
5. Where does that Person want to be according to Revelation 3:20 and how would you let Him in?

Do it:
Raj is a ten-year-old boy who is a bond servant. His master beats him daily. He often has to go without food and is very hungry. He feels that he is worthless. How could you use this introduction to encourage him?

* * * * *

Day Two: Christ in us . . .
the way to God.

"In the beginning was the Word . . ."
John 1:1

In order to understand the importance of Christ we first need to understand what it means to call Jesus the "Word of God." Words have two functions. They can be easily remembered by two words starting with the letter "r": <u>reveal</u> and <u>relate</u>. Words reveal us to each other and then relate us.

Although we have been married many decades, my wife still asks what I am thinking when I am silent for long periods. Although she is my life's partner she still cannot read my mind. I must speak in order for her to understand what is going on in my head. And if I refuse to talk, she doesn't know what I am thinking. My mind is hidden from her until I use words to tell her of my thoughts.

Words are necessary to reveal to others who we are. In this sinful world we can lie and thus disguise who we are. The Bible tells us that Satan is the father of all lies. He uses words to hide himself. But there is no shadow of deceit with God. And, wonder of wonders, God chooses to reveal Himself. Jesus, the second Person of the Trinity, is God's Word to us. And thus, He becomes the way to the Father. Jesus said, *"I am the way, the truth, and the life. No one comes to the Father except through Me" (John 14:6).*

How important is that function of being the WAY to the Father? The world lives in darkness, wondering Who God is. People create idols of wood and stone and bow down to worship lifeless gods. They live in darkness, fear, and superstition. How valuable is it to know the true, loving, perfect God? Knowing the truth about God is the single most valuable treasure we can possess. Now think that the One Who reveals God is knocking on your door, asking to come in and "eat" with you every day! How does the fact that the most important Person in the world is knocking at the door of our hearts right now, asking us to let Him in, affect you? If Jesus is so important, doesn't His presence in you give you new importance?

The second function of words is to <u>relate</u> us to one another. The most debilitating handicap is to be severely impaired in the areas of speech and hearing, for that cuts us off from all contact. It is utter, horrible loneliness not to be able to hear or speak. Words are bridges on which relationships are built. The Word of God, through revealing Who the Father is, builds many kinds of relationships with the Father for us. Here are some of them. He puts us "in" these relationships when He comes "into" us and lives in us. "If anyone is IN Christ he is a new creation" (2 Corinthians 5:17). To be "in" Christ is to be in these relationships:

1. **It is to be in a relationship like a branch to the vine**. *"I am the vine, you are the branches" (John 15:5)*.
2. **It is to be God's closest relative!** *"Behold, what manner of love the Father has lavished on us that we should be called children of God" (1 John 3:1)*.
3. **It is to be God's heirs**. *"Now if we are children, then we are heirs, heirs of God and co-heirs with Christ, if indeed we share in his sufferings in order that we may also share in his glory" (Romans 8:17)*.
4. **It is to be in, or a member of, the body of Christ**. *"Now you are the body of Christ, and each one of you is a part of it" (1 Corinthians 12:27)*.

5. **It is to be "tattooed" on the palms of God's hands**. *"See, I have engraved you on the palms of my hands" (Isaiah 49:16).* God loves us so much that He has our names on the "palms" of His hands!

How important do you think this Person is Who not only reveals to us the true nature of God the Father but also becomes the way to enter this multifaceted relationship with the Father? This little survey reveals the depth of the relationship with the Father through Jesus, a far deeper and more profound relationship than any other relationship. Remember . . . it is a relationship with the GREATEST, MOST IMPORTANT BEING IN THE UNIVERSE! And because Christ is in us we are as close to Him as a branch to its vine. We are called children of God, His heirs. We are called a part of Christ's body and we are engraved on His hands.

Learn it:

1. What are the two functions of words:

   R_____

   R_____

2. Since words are the foundation of all relationships, and Christ is the Word of God, then He becomes the foundation of our relationship with God. This relationship has many dimensions. We are related to Jesus as:

a. B _____ John 15: 5
b. C _____ I John 3:1
c. H _____ Romans 8:17
d. B _____ 1 Corinthians 12:27
e. T _____ Isaiah 49:16

3. How important is the Person Who relates us to God and where is He (Revelation 3:20)?

Do it:
How would you use this devotional, especially showing how Jesus relates us to God, to encourage Raj in his hard, discouraging life?

Prayer: Precious Savior, never let us forget how great and important You are as the Word of God. Thank You for revealing the Father to us. Thank You for relating us to Him and Yourself in so many intimate ways. In Your name we pray, Amen.

* * * * *

Day Three: Christ in us . . .
the greatness of God.

"In the beginning was the Word, and the Word
was with God, *and the Word was God . . . "*
John 1:1

Who is standing at our door each morning? How
great is this Person? How important is He?
Christ's greatness is shown in two ways. It is
shown in how high and exalted He is, and it is
shown in how He humbles Himself.

The greatness and the exaltedness of God is
shown in God's address to Job. God never
answered Job's problems. He merely impressed
on Job how high and powerful He is.

*"Who is this that darkens my counsel with words
without knowledge?*

Brace yourself like a man; I will question you, and
  you shall answer me.
Where were you when I laid the earth's foundation?
Tell me if you understand.
Who marked off its dimensions?
Surely you know!
Who stretched a measuring line across it?
On what were its footings set,
Or who laid its cornerstone—
While the morning stars [angels] sang together
And all the angels sang for joy?
Who shut up the sea behind doors when it burst
  forth from the womb?
When I made the clouds its garment and wrapped
  it in thick darkness,
When I fixed limits for it and set its doors and bars
  in place,
When I said, 'This far you may come and no farther;
Here is where your proud waves halt?'
Have you ever given orders to the morning or shown
  the dawn its place . . .

Job 38:2–12

  This passage deserves careful, slow, meditative
reading. God is so high, so majestic, so far beyond
us. Consider those questions God asked Job since
He is also asking them of us. Where were we when
He created the world and all the angels shouted for
joy? Did He consult with us to find

out how big and wide and wonderful all this should be? Of course He did not! Who is "knocking at our door" each morning wanting to come into us? It is this God, this great, awesome God. He wants to come into us spiritually through His Holy Spirit. How are we treating Him by the way we look at ourselves? We are saying He doesn't matter when we think we are nothing! Is it nothing to have the Creator God live in us? When we feel we are worthless and nothing, is there nothing in this God that is exciting enough to pull us out of a sense of failure? Is His love nothing to us? Does not His greatness give us a sense of importance?

But there is another aspect to His greatness expressed in Philippians 2:6–8.

"Who [Jesus], being in very nature God,
Did not consider equality with God something to
*   be grasped [held onto],*
But made Himself nothing,
Taking the very nature of a servant,
Being made in human likeness,
And being found in appearance as a man,
He humbled himself and became obedient to
*   death—even death on a cross!"*

If you think it is hard to fathom God's greatness as expressed in Job 38, then think of God's love. God's true greatness is expressed in His awesome love that enabled Christ to leave the glories of heaven and limit Himself to time and to our human nature. Christ became a human, while remaining God. Who can comprehend this? God is so great that His love penetrates to the deepest and lowest level. He comes not in great chariots but riding on the colt of a donkey! He comes not in majesty but in excruciating suffering and pain, dying an eternal death on Calvary's cross to pay for our sins.

Is it nothing that this amazing God literally stands before us each day, longing to come into us and go with us? Is His love and sacrifice so insignificant that it makes no difference in how we feel about ourselves? Yes, we have failed and we have sinned! But He loves us—and our value comes not from ourselves but from the fact that the greatest Being, the One Who stooped so low as to enter hell for us, now loves us so much that He longs to live *within us!*

Learn it:
1. List ways in which God's greatness is shown in nature (Job 38:2–12).
2. List the ways in which God's greatness is shown in His ability to "come down" as reflected in Philippians 2:6–8.
3. Which of these two forms of greatness is the "greatest"? Which one does Christ want to reveal through you by His presence in you according to Matthew 25:40?

Do it:
Raj, as a bond servant, is the lowest of the low. He is bound to his master until the family debt is paid. Jesus too became a "bond servant" and took upon Himself our punishment and paid it in full. In stooping down and serving He showed the real greatness of God. Explain how Raj can be a bond servant and yet in the low position of serving be like Jesus.

Prayer: Savior, make us stop. Set us apart from the business of our lives that keeps us from thinking about Your importance. Turn our eyes upon You, Jesus, and help us to see Your infinite importance and lift our spirits in joy and praise as we realize You want to live in us. Amen.

* * * * *

Day Four: Christ in us . . .
the knowledge of God.

"In the beginning was the Word,
and the Word was with God. *He was
with God in the beginning." John 1:1–2*

It was about noon on the day I suddenly lost sight
in my left eye. I looked up and there was a gray
shadow blocking my vision. I covered my right
eye and found that I could not see through my
left eye at all. I had suddenly and mysteriously
gone blind in one eye.

In the next days the doctors I saw were not
encouraging. They said that in some unknown
way the blood flow to the eye had been blocked
and I would never regain my sight. I certainly was
not planning on losing my sight! It was a giant
surprise. But it was no surprise for the One living

in me, for He is timeless. He has no beginning or no end. He lives outside of time. Everything is the present for Him. He knew the precise moment my sight would be taken away. We cannot understand eternity, for we are creatures of time, bound and locked between the past and the future. God lives in an eternal present. Forgetting much of the past and knowing nothing of the future we seem always to be surprised by current events, just as I was by the loss of the sight in my eye. Jesus has since shown His supernatural, miraculous power in restoring much of my vision in the damaged eye, in spite of the doctors telling me that I would never have use of it again!

This eternal Jesus lives and dwells in us. He knows everything about us. All of us are concerned about our hair. We wash it, comb it, set it, braid it, color it, are disturbed when it turns gray and even more upset when we lose it. As concerned as we are about our hair, there is one thing we don't know. We don't know how many hairs are on our head. But the One Who lives in us knows, for according to Matthew 10:30, "even the very hairs of your head are numbered. So don't be afraid!"

Jesus says something similar in Matthew 6:30-34. He tells us that our heavenly Father knows all our needs and as a good Father, He will supply. Jesus claims that He and the Father are One.

Now that Jesus dwells and lives in us, all our needs are known to Him! Surely if He loves us enough to live in us, we do not need to be afraid of anything, for He knows exactly what is going to happen. He is never afraid, for He sees everything at all times.

In Psalm 139:1–6 we find that Jesus knows us so well that He knows when we sit down and stand up and what we will say even before we say it. He is not outside of us, looking in or down on us. Christ is in us! His Spirit, the One Who searches the mind of God, now dwells in us and will reveal all truth to us (1 Corinthians 2:11).

Since God sees everything and there are no surprises He can assure us that He will make us to be more than conquerors according to Romans 8:37-39. To be more than conquerors means that nothing in all our life will be so great a surprise as to be able to separate us from the love of God.

What difference does it make to see Who Jesus is and where Jesus is? Jesus is not outside of us, or in heaven, nor is He like a light shining down on us. To all who believe, to all who trust Him, Jesus has promised to come in (Revelation 3:20) and be in us. Thus, as He pours His life into us, making us new creations, we never have to fear because Jesus is never surprised! He is timeless. He is eternal God. He sees everything and assures us that He is in total control.

Learn it:

1. The little cartoon at the beginning of this devotion illustrates how we are often surprised. What are some of the great surprises we face?

2. Why is Jesus, Who is God and thus eternal, never surprised by anything?

3. According to Matthew 6:31–34 what does God know about us, since He is eternal, and what should our attitude toward the future be?

4. How much does God know about us (Psalm 139:1–6)?

5. What does God know about our future (Romans 8:37–39)?

6. What difference should it make in our self-image that Jesus, Who is the eternal God, dwells in us?

Do it:

Raj has come to believe in Jesus and knows that Jesus, through His Holy Spirit, now lives in him. How can Raj have a good attitude toward the future because Jesus lives in him? Apply this lesson to Raj's life and show how it could help him.

Prayer: Precious Savior, grant that we may be aware of Your presence within us today and be comforted that You already see all the events not only of this day but of our life. May we be assured that there are no surprises and that because You live in us, nothing will ever separate us from Your love. For Your sake we pray, Amen.

* * * * *

Day Five: Christ in us . . .
the creating God.

"In the beginning was the Word and the Word
was with God and the Word was God. He
was with God in the beginning. *Through Him
all things were made; without Him nothing
was made that has been made . . . "*
John 1:3

Each of us has enough blood vessels in our body
that, if stretched out, they would circle the globe.
We have over 25,000 miles of veins, arteries, and
capillaries. These blood vessels are like highways
traveled every few seconds by 25 trillion to 30
trillion red blood cells. These blood cells live for
about 120 days. To replace those that wear out,

the bone marrow must produce about 200 billion new red cells daily, or 2 to 3 million every second, 24 hours a day! These cells are like little trucks and our lungs are the loading docks. Passing through the heart these little red trucks pause in the lungs, where they are loaded with oxygen, and when the heart beats they are sent throughout the body to every cell to bring that oxygen. When they unload it, each red blood cell picks up "garbage" (carbon dioxide) from the cell and as the heart beats again they race to the kidneys, where the waste from the cell is unloaded.

In addition to this amazing network of red cells the Creator put in white cells which are like police cars roaming through our body looking for "enemy" attacks in the form of disease. When they find disease or a wound they send out a call and these white cells fly into the area and attack the foreign intruders!

Not only do we not realize what is happening right within our own body, but we cannot understand what is happening in the universe. All of this came into existence, according to Genesis 1:3, because God spoke. God commanded everything that is, to be. John tells us that it was through Jesus, the Word of God, that all things were made. It was Jesus Who designed our bodies, including our red and white blood cells and the amazing system of blood vessels. It is through Jesus that the sun, moon, and stars were put in place.

Quiet streams lined with trees picture our Lord's love of beauty. What kinds of life are in the stream? How many fish make their home there? The endless scenes of nature reveal the greatness of our God. Massive trees grow from tiny shriveled and apparently dead seeds. Birds flit from tree to tree, each singing a distinctive song of praise. *This is the Creator God Who has chosen to live and dwell in us.* This is a most amazing truth. No wonder it is repeated over 160 times in the New Testament. "Christ in us, the hope of glory" (Colossians 1:27). "Christ lives in me!" (Galatians 2:20). Who is Christ? How important is He? The answer is that He is the One through Whom all things were made! He dwells in us through His Holy Spirit.

How can this be? Perhaps part of the answer is found in Genesis 1:26–27, the story of the creation of Adam. God determined that humans would be created in "our image and our likeness." While we are NOT God, we are His closest "relatives." He created us superior even to the angels, for they are God's servants while we are God's children. God adopts us as His children and heirs. Perhaps this is why Christ, through His Holy Spirit, can dwell in us. We were made to be God's friends. We were made to have a living relationship with Him. We were made to be branches on the vine of Christ so that His life flows through us.

What does having the Creator of the universe live in you do for your sense of value? How does the fact that the Creator of all things, the One through Whom all things were made, now dwells in us make us feel about ourselves?

Prayer: Savior, these concepts are so staggering, so awesome that we cannot even start to understand them. How can we, who do not even know the mysteries and miracles of our own bodies, nor understand the stars and planets, begin to appreciate Your glory and power and majesty? With tears of joy we bow before You, Lord. How can it be that You should so honor us that You stand before our door daily, knocking and asking if You may come in? How can it be that we are so busy with such trivial concerns that often we do not hear Your knock at the door and in our haste fail to include You in our lives that day? Forgive us. Cleanse us. And grant us the overwhelming experience of Your presence today. For Your sake we pray, Jesus. Amen.

Learn it:
1. What happened when God spoke (Genesis 1:3) and how does this show the amazing power of God?
2. What is special about the way God created humans according to Genesis 1:26, 27?

- What does being created this way mean for your self-worth?
- For your self-image?
- For your self-purpose?
3. What characteristic of all of God's creation is found in Genesis 1:31 and what does this mean?
4. What does having the Creator of everything living in you do for you?

Do it:

How would the understanding that the "Creator of Everything" now lives in Raj, help him in his daily difficulties? How would it give him new dignity? How would it give him hope?

* * * * *

Day Six: Christ in us . . .
the life-giving God.

"In the beginning was the Word, and the Word was with God and the Word was God. He was with God in the beginning. Through Him all things were made; without Him nothing was made that has been made. *In Him was life and that life was the light of men.*" John 1:4

Nothing is more important to us than life. We are consumed with living. We eat to live. We work to provide food to eat. We sleep to live. When we get sick we are concerned that we will die.

Christ, according to John 1:4, is the author of all life. Jesus claimed that title for Himself when, standing before a distraught sister whose brother

Lazarus had died, said, "I am the resurrection and the life. He who believes in me will live, even though he dies; and whoever lives and believes in me will never die. Do you believe this?" (John 11:25–26).

While scientists understand many things, the mystery of life still escapes them. We can paint a picture of a flower, and we can build a model flower, but we cannot create a real flower. No one fully understands the mystery of life contained in a flower seed. That little seed, so hard, planted in moist earth and bathed with sunlight, bursts into a new plant that in time produces a glorious flower. All over planet earth, our Savior graces the landscape with a multitude of varieties of flowers.

He assures us, that since He lives in us through faith, whoever believes in Him will never die. That means that we have eternal life planted in us beginning the moment we believe in Christ. That life will not die, for Christ is the author of that life. He tells us that as we remain in Him and He remains in us, we as the branches receiving His life will bear much fruit. While our bodies will die, they are like seeds, shriveled and hard. They are planted in the earth and when Jesus comes again, they will spring to life. However, our bodies then will be like flowers are to the seeds from which they came! They will be infinitely more glorious. They will be heavenly bodies.

Praise the Savior. Bow humbly before this awesome God, knowing that He loves us so much that He has made us His dwelling place. When you think of the fact that "Christ lives in me" remember these five truths:

- He is the One Who reveals Who God is and relates us to our Father. He is the only Way to the Father and He lives in us!
- He is the One Who shows us the greatness of God in creation but far more shows us the love of God in His sacrifice for our sins. This God lives in us!
- He is the One Who is the beginning and the end. He is timeless, eternal. There are no surprises for our Savior. And He lives in us!
- He is the Creator of all things and He is the One Who made us in His image. And He lives in us!
- He is the Source of all life and the Source of life lives in us, assuring us that as we trust Him we will never die. Praise His name forever!

Learn it:
1. Who is the Creator of all life?
2. How does Jesus describe Himself in John 11:25 and what do you think that means?
3. In the rank of all beings, how important is the Creator of all life?

4. How close are we to the Creator of life according to John 15:1-5?

5. List the five descriptions of Christ in this lesson according to John 1:1–4. Explain what difference it makes to know that this Person is knocking at your door daily, asking to be included in your life.

Do it:

Review each of the five descriptions of Christ by applying them to Raj's life. Show how each of these five descriptions can help Raj not only face his daily struggle but also give him hope of finding a better life.

Prayer: Precious Savior, may we have an entirely new attitude toward ourselves in the light of the wonder that You now live in us. May we see the value You give us. May the light of Your presence stream into every part of our being, cleansing us from sin. May it then stream out, drawing all people to You. May we experience Your loving presence in freeing us from all fear and giving us vision, courage, and power. In Your name we pray, Jesus, Amen.

* * * * *

Day Seven: Reflection

1. What did you like about the devotions this week?
2. Was there anything that you did not like or did not understand?
3. What unique new lessons did you learn about God?
4. Did this lesson help you in any practical way. Explain how.

Week Three:

"Our New Power to Forgive"

"But while he was still a long way off, his father saw him and was filled with compassion for him; he ran to his son." Luke 15:20

"For just as through the disobedience of the one man the many were made sinners, so also through the obedience of the one man the many will be made righteous." Romans 5:19

"Quick! Bring the best robe and put it on him. Put a ring on his finger and sandals on his feet!" Luke 15:22

"Forgive us our sins as we forgive those who sin against us." Matthew 6:12

Day One: Introduction

We have seen the importance of the One Who lives in us. He is the only Way to know God and be loved by our Father. He reveals Who God is and relates us to God. He shows us God's greatness not merely in creation but much more in God's ability to stoop down to love us. He is never surprised because He is eternal. He is the Creator of all that exists and is the Source of all life.

If so great a Being lives in us **there is awesome power at our disposal**. Jesus told us we would do greater works than He did! *"I tell you the truth, anyone who has faith in me will do what I have been doing. He will do even greater things than these, because I am going to the Father" (John 14:12)*.

We have been emphasizing that Jesus is in us, spiritually. Christ is also with the Father in heaven. He is present everywhere since He is God. He is especially present in us, through His Holy Spirit. Since His Spirit is in us, His power dwells in us.

One of the greatest demonstrations of Christ's power occurred as He was nailed to the cross. It is the power to forgive. As the nails were being driven into His hands and feet and the cross was raised in place, He prayed that His Father would forgive those who were doing this horrible thing. That same forgiving power is now flowing through us because He lives in us. Family fights are stopping as His power to forgive flows through His new disciples. Quarreling is ceasing. In place of hatred, there is love. In place of self-ishness there is selfless sacrifice. In place of blind-ness to others' needs there is tender and compassionate sight. While Christ demonstrated this in His life in Palestine for thirty-three years, it is now being demonstrated worldwide through all His believers. Far greater works of forgiveness are being demonstrated all over the world!

This week we meditate on five aspects of the power to forgive, which is a most precious power of our Savior.

1. **The time** when forgiveness occurs. We will see how quickly and eagerly our Father grants salvation to us.
2. **The eagerness** of the Father to forgive.

3. The amazing results of being forgiven by God.
4. The reason why we can be forgiven.
5. The unique power of Christ enabling us to forgive others.

Learn it:

1. Make up a story of forgiveness based on this picture. Tell who these people are, what might have happened to them, what is going on, and what the light symbolizes about the situation.
2. The five "powers" of Christ displayed in forgiveness and being forgiven are:

   1. The _____ when forgiveness occurs.
   2. The _____ to of the Father to forgive.
   3. The amazing _____ of being forgiven.
   4. The _____ why we can be forgiven.
   5. We will experience _____ to forgive others.

3. What promise of power is given in John 14:12?
4. Where is that Power (John 15:5)? Why is being forgiven and forgiving others one of the greatest displays of power?

Do it:

Terrorists came into the village, killed Selvi's parents, and then took her to their camp. They mistreated her badly, beating her daily. They hardly gave her enough to eat and she lost weight and became very sick. Yet Selvi showed a spirit of forgiveness and love to them. Can you explain how she could forgive them?

* * * * *

Day Two: God's power displayed at the time when forgiveness occurs.

"But while he was still a long way off . . . "
Luke 15:20

This story, recorded in Luke 15, is a very unusual one. Part of the story was very well known, told often by the rabbis of Jesus day. But the ending Christ put on it was radically different. Instead of having the father disown the wayward son, Jesus gave the story an amazing twist, saying that the father was waiting on the road for his wayward son to come home. Each day he went out. With great longing he looked far into the distance to see if his son was returning. Often called the parable of the Prodigal Son, this story is really about the Forgiving Father.

It is a story about the God's power to forgive. The *time* when the father forgave his son is important. It was when he was still *"a long way off."* We often insist that in order to be forgiven a person must first make amends. We want the person to return all the way! But God doesn't demand this of us. He has made it all right through the death of Jesus His Son. All He asks is for is a basic decision to turn around and *start* to walk back to Him. He doesn't measure the distance we have come in order to forgive us. He only sees that we have turned back toward home.

In God's forgiveness even motives need not be pure. This son returned home not because he wanted to apologize for hurting his father, but because he was starving and figured his father's servants were better off than he was. It was the misery of his condition that drove him to turn. But that was overlooked by the father.

The father was only concerned that his son had turned toward home. Nothing else mattered, and while he was still a long, long way away he rushed to him. This is a tremendous comfort for all of us. We have all sinned. God doesn't wait until we prove ourselves. He, like the father in Jesus' story, is waiting for us and sees us while we are a long way off. What incredible power is displayed in being willing to forgive us while we are still a long way away from Him.

Learn it:

1. Make up a story about forgiveness based on this picture. What are the parents looking for?

Do you think they will wait for their son to return, or will they run to meet him?

2. According to Luke 15:20 what did the son do to begin the process of forgiveness?

3. When did the father respond and offer forgiveness? Was it after the boy returned all the way home, or just as he started to return? What does this tell us about our Father in heaven?

4. What were the boy's motives in returning home? Were they a selfish concern for himself or a selfless concern for the father? What does this tell us about God's willingness to forgive us?

Do it:
Sam never felt God fully forgave him for his sins. He always felt that God was still angry with him. How would you use this devotional to assure Sam of God's full forgiveness?

Prayer: Father, help us to see Your awesome power of forgiveness that even while we are still very far from You, You see us and come to us. How we praise You, Lord, that You accept us in all our sin and misery as this boy was accepted. May we be thrilled in Your awesome power to receive us just as we are. For Jesus' sake, Amen.

* * * * *

Day Three: God's power is displayed in His eagerness to forgive.

"But while he was still a long way off his father saw him and was filled with compassion for him; *he ran to his son threw his arms around him and kissed him . . .* " Luke 15:20

The father's eagerness to forgive is so great that it forces him to run toward this son who had sinned against him so badly. The picture of the "running" father is very important. Fathers in Jesus' time did not run. It was undignified. They especially did not run to greet someone who had sinned against them as badly as this son had sinned. He had shown no consideration for his father's feelings. He had dishonored the family name. He had demanded his inheritance before his father died and thus displayed his hard-hearted selfishness. There probably is not a human father who would have been willing to forgive such a sinful son, much less **run** to greet that son as he started to return.

All of us are very reluctant to forgive. It is hard to forgive. We nurture our hurt feelings. We enjoy thoughts of revenge. We delight in making our enemies crawl. We refuse to speak to those who once were closest to us because of the pain we have endured. We want to protect ourselves, we say, from being hurt again.

Nurturing hatred is like nurturing a spiritual cancer. The resulting bitterness will spread and kill. Christ came to set us free from the bondage of hate and revenge. And that freedom begins by realizing the power of the heavenly Father to forgive us as illustrated in this story. Forgiveness starts while the boy is a *long way away,* and expresses itself in the rather undignified running toward him. The father doesn't wait to find out the boy's motives or to see if the repentance is genuine. He is so eager for forgiveness and restitution that he "flies" to embrace his long-lost son.

Since Christ is in us, this is the kind of power for forgiveness that is flowing through us. As we rejoice in God's eagerness to forgive us, we can also rejoice in our new eagerness to let that forgiveness flow through us to those who have hurt us. True forgiveness from God always overflows in forgiveness of others.

Let's remember that as we study God's power to forgive us. God's power to forgive us is the same power that enables us to forgive others! What we cannot do, God can do. We are Christ's body and we are to release His forgiving power in our forgiving others. The first and most important form of Christ's power is our willingness to forgive and be reconciled to each other.

Learn it:

1. People lacking Christ's _____ to forgive are very reluctant to forgive. Why do we need Christ's supernatural, mysterious, inexplicable power to forgive others?

2. God is _____ to forgive us. Why do we find this hard to believe?

3. God is so eager to forgive us that He does not _____ for us to come all the way back to Him, but _____ to us while we are still a long way off.

4. The Father's eagerness is so great that He is willing to lose His _____ in running to receive us.

Do it:

John felt that he would never forgive the men who had hurt his child. He bore bitterness and hatred in his heart for many years. He was not a believer in Jesus. His religion taught revenge and hatred as the only way of settling scores. He was startled to learn that God was eager to forgive him. How would God's eagerness to forgive him help him forgive others? What did John have to look forward to by forgiving those who hurt him so much?

Prayer: Savior we praise and adore You for revealing to us the eagerness of our Father in heaven to forgive and restore us. Thank You for this picture of the running Father Who sees us while we are still far away in our sin but turning back to Him. We praise You that He runs to greet us and embraces us and welcomes us. In Your name, Savior, we pray, Amen.

* * * * *

Day Four: God's power is pictured in the result of forgiveness.

"But while he was still a long way off, his father saw him and was filled with compassion for him; he ran to his son, threw his arms around him and kissed him. *Quick! Bring the best robe and put it on him. Put a ring on his finger and sandals on his feet!*" Luke 15:20–22

Nice clothes make us feel good; they improve our self-image. Perhaps no other nation on earth provides such elegant clothing for women as does the nation of India. The bride at her wedding is clothed in the richest garments parents can buy and adorned with gold jewelry. In the West, brides spend huge sums of money on wedding dresses. Men rent special wedding clothes.

Nothing does so much for one's self-image and sense of value, however, as the robes that God puts on us after He has forgiven us. One of the most beautiful descriptions of these robes is found in Isaiah 61:10. "*I delight greatly in the Lord; my soul rejoices in my God. For he has clothed me with garments of salvation and arrayed me in a robe of righteousness, as a bridegroom adorns his head like a priest, and as a bride adorns herself with jewels."*

As we picture Christ living in us we should be delighted. People who get dressed up for a wedding are excited. This is their finest moment. Isaiah tells us that God has dressed us up in wedding clothes! Because we are clothed in Christ's righteousness we can be forgiven. We are not dirty any longer in our Father's sight. He has placed the "robes of righteousness" on us. These are "white" robes (Revelation 6:11). Our spirits should soar as we try to imagine how beautiful we look to our Father, dressed in the perfect robes of His only Son.

But forgiveness doesn't merely give us new, spiritual clothing. God gives us a ring, the family ring. In Jesus' day, the ring was a symbol of authority, just as it still is in monarchies. The king's seal or ring, stamped on documents, makes them official. When Christ becomes our representative, covering us with His perfect obedience and His eternal death for our sins, then the Father immediately restores us to a position of great authority. This is described in Matthew 18:18. *"I tell you the truth, whatever you bind on earth will be bound in heaven, and whatever you loose on earth will be loosed in heaven."* Because Christ is in us, His authority is in us. We can, in the name of Jesus Who lives in us, bind evil spirits. Since Christ is "in" us and we are "in" Him, having taken Him as our new Head and representative, we now share in His authority. That authority is expressed in these words. *"And having disarmed the powers and authorities, he made a public spectacle of them, triumphing over them by the cross" (Colossians 2:15)*. Jesus has defeated all the demonic spirits and that Jesus lives "in" us who believe in Him! We must not walk around and act as if we are defeated! The evil spirits are the defeated ones, not us.

Finally, the father puts sandals on the son's feet. This is a symbol that the wayward son has been restored to full status in the family. He is a true child of his father. And this is what God does for us through the power of forgiveness. *"Behold, what manner of love the Father has lavished on us that we should be called children of God and such we are" (I John 3:1)*.

Think of what God's forgiveness involves! He is waiting so eagerly for us to turn in faith to Him that He pictures Himself as running to us. He has paid the ultimate price in the death of His own Son in order to forgive us! After such a price it is understandable that He would run to forgiveness. There is no greater display of power in the whole universe than the power God showed in making His Only Begotten Son our second representative. He clothes us with the greatest garments in the world, the robes of righteousness.

He puts the ring of His authority on our finger and He puts sandals on our feet as a sign of His lavish love in adopting us as His children.

This is the basis of a total transformation of our sense of value, our picture of ourselves, and our sense of purpose in life!

Learn it:
1. Explain what happens when Christ forgives us for our sins.
   - What does the robe stand for (Isaiah 61:10)?
   - What does the ring represent (Matthew 18:18)?
   - What do the sandals represent (I John 3:1)?
2. How far does God remove our sins when He forgives us (Psalm 103:12)? What do you think this means?
3. How does Isaiah 1:18 picture God's power to forgive? What does this mean for you?
4. Why should the feeling expressed in Romans 5:1–2 be the feeling we have when we are forgiven?

Do it:
Joythi had stolen from her parents and dishonored her family name. She had also lived a very immoral and sinful life. Joythi had great difficulty, even after she became a believer, in forgetting her sinful past. How could this devotion help her?

Prayer: Our Father, we never fully have understood the power You displayed in providing salvation by giving us Your only Son as our new representative. You allowed Him to become one of us. Jesus, You did not hold on to Your exalted position, but limited Yourself not only to our human form but also to time. We cannot comprehend the power this took. And then as a human, You bore eternal punishment for all Your followers so that our Father could freely and eagerly forgive us! May we see ourselves clothed in Your perfect righteousness, Jesus, with Your ring of authority on our finger and Your family shoes on our feet. In Your precious name, Jesus. Amen.

* * * * *

Day Five: God's power shown in the basis of forgiveness.

"For just as through the disobedience of the one man [Adam—our first representative] the many were made sinners, so also through the obedience of the one man [Jesus—our second representative] the many will be made righteous."
Romans 5:19

There is something very unsettling about the story of the father that we have studied. It just doesn't seem right. The son has brought such dishonor to the family and hurt the father so much. Shouldn't something be done to make things right? How can this father ignore all that has been done wrong and run to greet this son and throw his arms around this filthy boy?

Remember that Jesus is telling this story with a double meaning. It is not merely a story about an earthly father. It is a story that reveals the truth about our heavenly Father and His eagerness to forgive us. What Jesus does not explain in the story is why the Father is so eager to forgive us. Why can He forgive us? What is the basis of His forgiveness? What is the reason behind His running to us? How can He offer to forgive us?

No other area shows God's love and power as clearly as His ability to forgive us. He Himself has made everything right between us through His Son Jesus Christ. Paul explains this in Romans 5. He points out that when God created humans He gave us a representative to act for us. That representative was the first human, Adam. And Adam failed. Adam sinned and plunged the human race into sin. God was not defeated. He provided a second representative to act for us, Jesus Christ, His only Son.

Through Adam's sin against God death came to everyone because Adam represented everyone and chose sin. *"For if by the trespass of one man, death reigned [over all] through that one man, how much more will those who receive God's abundant provision of grace and of the gift of righteousness reign in life through the one man, Jesus Christ"* (Romans 5:17). Jesus was given to us as our second representative. He not only was perfectly obedient to God (sinless) and thus provided a perfect righteousness for all who chose Him as their representative, but He also provided a complete punishment for all our sins when He died on the cross. This was a legal punishment. He was not murdered but was executed as a criminal, even though He was sinless. In that death He fulfilled our punishment. He didn't have to die for Himself. He died for us. Thus God our Father, by providing us with a second representative Who gave the perfect obedience Adam failed to give, and Who also paid our eternal punishment for sin, now sets before us the choice of which representative we want to follow.

When we trust Jesus and believe in Him, we "elect" Him as our representative. He acts for us. *"For just as through the disobedience of the one man [Adam—our first representative] the many were made sinners, so also through the obedience of the one man [Jesus—our second representative] the many will be made righteous" (Romans 5:19).*

To have Christ "in" us means that when we, by faith in Jesus, vote to have Him represent us, we are totally, completely covered by His perfect obedience and His eternal payment of our sins. Realizing that Jesus now represents us, and we are "in" Him and He is "in" us brings about a profound transformation in our sense of value, self-image, and purpose in life! We have been set free!

God's eagerness to forgive us is easily understood when we grasp the concept that Jesus is our second representative and He cleared the way through His life and His sacrificial death. Why wouldn't our Father be eager to forgive us after allowing His Son to suffer and die on our behalf? Why wouldn't such a Father be standing on the road, looking for our return with great eagerness, and running to greet us when He sees us in the distance?

Learn it:

1. A representative is someone who_____ on our behalf. He r_____ us.
2. We have a choice of two representatives: A_____ or C_____
3. To be "in" Christ means that we are being r_____ by Him.
   - This means His perfect obedience belongs to _____ and becomes our perfect obedience.
   - This means that His p_____ for sin through His death on the cross becomes our punishment for sin!
4. "I was crucified with Christ and I no longer live but Christ lives in me" (Galatians 2:20). Explain this verse in the light of your answers to questions 2 and 3.
5. Why, in the light of the tremendous work of Jesus, is the Father so eager to forgive us?

Do it:

Ruth found it impossible to forgive her parents. They had abused her and beaten her. They constantly degraded her, preferring that she would have been a son rather than a daughter. And yet, by understanding this devotion, Ruth was able to forgive her parents, love them, and care for them. How could the truth taught today do this for Ruth?

Prayer: Thank You, Lord Jesus, for becoming our new representative. Thank You that we can be covered with Your perfection and through Your punishment be cleansed of all our sin. May we always abide in You and have You abide in us. Grant that we may rejoice in realizing that You are powerful enough to make a way to completely take away all our sin and give us forgiveness as a complete and free gift. In Your name, Jesus, we pray, Amen.

* * * * *

Day Six: God's power is shown in our NEW ability to forgive.

"Forgive us our sins as we forgive those who sin against us." Matthew 6:12
(Read: Matthew 18:21–35)

Every person on earth experiences broken relationships and the need to offer forgiveness. If forgiveness is the greatest display of God's power, and if Jesus Christ, the One in Whom that power is displayed, lives in us, then we should be marvelous examples of forgiveness as well. Satan realizes that the more we show forgiveness to those who have wronged us, the more Jesus' power of forgiveness is revealed through us. Satan's primary tools to keep us in sin are the tools of revenge, bitterness, and hatred. The one thing Satan hates the most is a forgiving disciple of Jesus.

Most people do not understand the benefits of being able to forgive those who sin against us. Here are some examples.

- First, when we forgive others we are assured that we are "sons" of God. Jesus told us that "peacemakers" are especially blessed, for "they will be called sons of God" (Matthew 5:9). Peacemakers are people who offer forgiveness. Having both experienced and understood the forgiveness God has given, they know they **have no choice** but to forgive those who have sinned against them.
- Second, when we forgive those who persecute us we have great "reward" in heaven. Jesus says that when people persecute us and say all manner of false lies about us, we should be glad because we will have a "great reward" in heaven (Matthew 5:11-12). Jesus is saying that every time we are hurt by someone else, we have a new opportunity to allow His power to flow from within us in forgiveness of that person. How much we have been wronged and hurt does not matter; Christ's power to forgive is infinite. We are to forgive in Christ's power, not our own.
- Third, forgiving others is one of the most freeing and liberating experiences. When we harbor

thoughts of revenge we are nurturing a kind of spiritual cancer that enslaves us to hatred. Jesus says that hatred is a form of murder (Matthew 5:21–24). It keeps us from true worship. Jesus says if there is any problem with another person we must get it solved immediately. When we are consumed with hatred and feel we will never be able to forgive, we must remember Galatians 2:20. *"I was crucified with Christ and I no longer live but Christ lives in me."* By refusing to forgive, we are living as the old person we were! But Christ lives in us and He is the One Who has the ultimate power, the power to forgive. The first way in which we are set free, when Christ comes into us, is by getting rid of the heavy burden of hatred and revenge. When we forgive those who have sinned against us we are liberated!

- Finally, offering forgiveness is the necessary response to being forgiven. In Matthew 18: 21–35 Jesus tells the parable of a servant who was forgiven a massive debt but in return refused to forgive a very small debt owed to him. Jesus points out in the parable that we have no choice but to forgive when we are forgiven for a lifetime of sin. Forgiving others is the result of being transformed to wear robes of righteousness and the ring of God's authority and call ourselves children of the King of Forgiveness. *We must forgive those who have sinned against us.* The point of the story is that no one could possibly have sinned against us as we have sinned against God. Having been forgiven so much, surely we must in turn forgive what others have done against us. We are able to do this because the Power of Forgiveness, our Lord Jesus, dwells in us and it is in His power that we can forgive others.

Learn it:
1. What does this picture tell you about forgiving one another?
2. Why is it hard to forgive each other? Suggest several reasons.
3. How necessary is it to forgive according to Matthew 6:12?
4. How does Christ's power in us enable us to forgive according to the story in Matthew 18:21–35? What did the unmerciful servant forget? How does concentration on the presence of Christ in us enable us not to forget this?

Do it:
The three boys were deserted by their parents and left alone to live on the streets, begging and stealing to get food. They became very hard and filled with hatred. They went to a Children's Bible Club and found out how much God suffered in giving His Son as our representative to pay the

punishment for our sins. How did that discovery set them free from the bitterness they felt against their parents for abandoning them?

Prayer: Savior, as we have experienced Your forgiveness this week, enable us to be channels of that great power to forgive. May Your forgiving power flow through us in reconciling us with those whom we have offended and who have offended us. Let Your strength take over, Savior, and motivate and move us to show Your love to them in asking and offering forgiveness. We pray it in the power of Your name alone, Amen.

* * * * *

Day Seven: Reflection

1. What did you like about the devotions this week?
2. Was there anything that you did not like or did not understand?
3. What unique new lessons did you learn about God?
4. Did this lesson help you in any practical way? Explain how.

Week Four

"Our New Power to Change"

"I am the vine; you are the branches. If a man remains in me and I in him, he will bear much fruit; apart from me you can do nothing. If anyone does not remain in me, he is like a branch thatis thrown away and withers . . ."
John 15:5, 6

Introduction:

The desire for change: When I was a little boy I never wanted to go to heaven. Heaven sounded boring because everything was perfect. I didn't think there would ever be any change and that sounded terrible. I was wrong. The Bible tells us that heaven will be full of eternal growth (change). It says "But now abides faith, hope and love . . ." (1 Corinthians 13:13). Hope, along with faith and love, is eternal. Hope is looking forward to change. Heaven will be eternal exploration and growth into the beauty of a God Who has no limits. There will be constant, wonderful change as we continually discover new wonders of God's power and majesty. We will always be looking forward to new discoveries of God's greatness. Since heaven is eternal life, and life is always expressed in growth, and growth means change, there will be change in heaven.

The joy of change: Think of little children. None of us would ever want our children to remain the same. The thrill of having children is watching them grow through the various stages of life. To be alive is to be growing. Change keeps us all going. We want to change our lives for the better. We want to change our families, our neighborhoods, our villages, and our states and nations all for the better. We want our businesses to "grow" and change for the better. It is the longing for change for something better that drives us all. Changing and improving things gives life meaning and purpose.

The power for change: We can see the power of change when we compare a small seed to the tree which grows from it. No one can fully understand how an apparently dead, hard seed, when placed in the ground and watered, can sprout, reaching up above the ground. There, warmed by the sun and watered by the rain, that little sprout arising out of the seed begins to change. First it appears as a little seedling, and then a little stem with a few branches. Over the next months and years it grows into a huge, massive tree. What made that little seed change so much? It is the power of life.

The formula for change: While we can work hard to bring about transformation, spiritual change within us can come only through the life of Jesus flowing into us and through us. That life of Jesus, as we see in our text this week, will flow and expand in us only when "**He remains in us and we remain in Him.**" In other words, just as a seed must be put in the ground in order to germinate and grow into a tree, so also we must meet the condition of remaining in Christ in order to have the life of Christ grow in us.

Remaining in Christ can be done through daily praying the "New You" prayer. We should pray it each morning when we awaken. We should start each day asking,

Q: "Where are You, Jesus?" and listen for His answer: "I am in you…"

Q: "Who are You, Jesus?" and He will answer: "I am the light of the world…"

Q: "What do you want me to do today, Jesus?" His answer will be: "I want you to turn on My light and let it shine out of you."

By asking "Where are You, Jesus?" we remind ourselves that Jesus is not only outside of us but, more importantly, Jesus is in us. Understanding what it means to have Jesus in us transforms our sense of self-worth.

In asking "Who are You, Jesus?" we remind ourselves that the most important, powerful, beautiful Person in the universe has chosen to live and dwell in our lives. When we look "in" and see Jesus, our self-image is transformed. There is something beautiful inside us. We have infinite value because Jesus is in us and His "value" cannot be measured. It is limitless. When we ask, "What do you want today, Jesus?" we remind ourselves of the tremendous purpose Christ gives us for living. We are to let His light shine from within us. That light is life. Jesus' life in us produces supernatural change and growth similar to the change of a seed into a massive tree. The key to transforming change lies in remaining in Christ so His life can flow through us, producing eternal fruit. When we forget our place in Christ, and try to change and transform ourselves without His power, we can do nothing.

Learn it:
1. Why does growth always bring change?
2. What happens when we stop hoping for something better?
3. When does change bring joy?

4. How do these pictures illustrate the power needed for true change?
5. What are the three parts of the prayer for change?

Do it:

Meditate today on the "New You" prayer. Remind yourself of the three important thoughts that will transform your sense of value and give you a new image:

- Jesus is in me.
- Jesus is the light of the world.
- Jesus wants to shine out of me.

Picture yourself as the house glowing with warm light in the darkness because that is a picture of being "born again."

* * * * *

Day Two: "Where are You, Jesus?"

"I am the vine; you are the branches." John 15:5

It took me a long time to understand the answer to the question, "Where are You, Jesus?" I, as many Christians, thought of Jesus as someone "outside" of me. He is in heaven, or at best, walking beside us, or even carrying us. A careful reading of the New Testament, however, indicates that the relationship we have with Jesus is far more intimate. Jesus *is inside* of us. "I was crucified with Christ and I no longer live but Christ lives in me" (Galatians 2:20). Jesus, the most important Person in the universe, pictures Himself as standing at the door of our hearts, knocking like a common servant. He wants to come in. *"Here I am! I stand at the door and knock. If anyone hears my voice and opens the door, I will come in and eat with him, and he with me"* (Revelation 3:20).

Whenever I looked "inside" myself all I saw was failure. I became depressed even though I was a Christian. I thought of Jesus as the light shining down on me, but inside I found very little that I liked. And then that glorious moment occurred when I was challenged with this question, "Where is the light, John? Where is the light?" I suddenly realized that the light was inside of me. I pictured Christ's beauty and Perfection *as something inside of me!* Suddenly I had a new attitude toward myself. If, indeed, Christ lives in me then there is something inside of which I can be proud. If all I see when I look inside is "me," then I am insulting my Savior. I am sinning against Him. I must build my attitude on what the Bible teaches me about Jesus living in me. Who are we when Jesus dwells in us?

We are His branches! *"I am the vine; you are the branches"(John 15:5).*

As we begin each day we must remind ourselves that since Christ lives in us, He makes us to be His branches. A branch produces flowers and fruit. It is the expression of the life which flows through the vine. As Jesus lives in us, pouring His life into us, He is the One Who will produce the flowers and the fruit in our lives. We need to remind ourselves that we are not on our own, running our own lives with a little help from above! When we desperately want to change, to become better and more beautiful, to sin less and obey more, to overcome selfishness with selflessness, we need to remind ourselves that we are branches. We must remember that Jesus lives *in us* and that the life we now live is His life. He is the One Who can make an acorn grow to be an oak tree and He is the One Who can bring glorious change in us when we remain in Him.

We are His body! *"Now you are the body of Christ, and each one of you is a part of it"* (1 Corinthians 12:27).

Where is Jesus? He tells us that we are His body and He is our head. That means that while He is a Spirit and no one can see Him, He uses us to show others what He is like. A group of businessmen were hurrying to catch a train when one of them knocked over a stand of fruit in the marketplace and scattered apples all over the ground. The men hurried on, paying no attention. Suddenly one stopped. He told the others to go ahead and catch the train. He turned back and picked up the damaged fruit. He then paid the vendor, who was a young blind boy, for the fruit that was damaged. As he was leaving the blind boy called out, "Hey, mister, is your name Jesus?"

As we start each day we pray, "Where are You, Jesus?" and our Savior replies, "I am in you. You are not only My branches but you are My body."

We are His building! *"Don't you know that you yourselves are God's temple and that God's Spirit lives in you? And if anyone destroys God's temple,*

God will destroy him; for God's temple is sacred, and you are that temple" (1 Corinthians 3:16, 17).

Because Jesus lives in us He not only makes us His branches and His body, but also His "building" or His dwelling place. Temples are the homes of the gods. Jesus says He does not live in a stone temple or a building but lives in us, His disciples. We become His sacred dwelling place. Jesus is the light of the world. His presence in us makes us the light of the world, as He shines out of us. When we sin we pull the shades down and His light cannot shine. Remember the picture with which we started? We are glowing because Christ has made us His dwelling place!

Learn it:

1. What is the first prayer we should offer in the morning as we build a new self-image?

2. How does Christ answer this prayer (Revelation 3:20)?

3. When Christ lives in us we become His

   B_____

   B_____

   B_____

4. Why do those three things change your sense of value and your self-image?

5. In what way does each one affect your purpose in life?

Do it:

Jim was fired from his job. His boss had it in for him and abused him. Finally the antagonism got so bad that the boss laid him off. Jim has four children. Because he was fired he now has difficulty getting another job. He doesn't know how to feed his four children. How could Jim apply this lesson to help him in this situation?

Prayer: We praise You, Savior, that You are in us! And that being in us You transform us to be Your branches, Your body, Your building in which You live. Grant that we may be changed by Your life flowing into us and through us. May growth be as great a transformation as a seed growing to be a tree. We praise You that Your life in us is eternal life. We praise You that forever we will grow and change into Your likeness and Your beauty. For Your sake we pray, Amen.

* * * * *

Day Three: "Who are You, Jesus?"

"I am the vine and you are the branches. *If a man remains in me and I in him . . .*" John 15:5

The power for change comes when we remain in Christ by starting each day with the prayer "Where are You, Jesus?" We remain in Christ when we remind ourselves that He is in us making us His branches, body, and building. We remain in Christ when we remind ourselves of Who Jesus is and draw our value from Him, not from what we do or own or what others say about us. Remaining in Christ consists of focusing our mind on Christ, not on ourselves.

In the second week we pictured ourselves as being in the White House of the president of the United States, or in the home of the prime minister. We asked ourselves what would happen to our self-worth if we would be able to meet each week with the leader of our nation. That meeting will never occur for most of us. However, something of infinitely more importance does happen each morning when we remind ourselves of WHO it is that lives in us. It is not enough to merely ask where Jesus is, we must remind ourselves of the importance of Jesus. Let's review what we learned in John 1:1–4.

"In the beginning was the Word…" Jesus is the most important Being in the universe because He is the only Person Who can reveal Who God is. He is the Word or revelation of God. In revealing God to us, Jesus relates us to God. Words relate us to each other. Unless we know what is on each other's mind we cannot form bonds of love and friendship. Jesus is the Father's way of speaking to us so that we can come to know the Father and be adopted as His children. As you start the day, remember that Jesus is God's Word, God's revelation of Himself. No other person or angel is more important than this, and this is the Person Who lives in us!

"And the Word was with God and the Word was God." As we ask "Who are You, Jesus?" we must remember that Jesus is God. The Bible reveals the mystery that while there is only One God, that God exists as three equal Persons,

Father, Son, and Holy Spirit. Jesus was given to us, as our representative. While remaining God He was also human. He acted for us by giving the Father sinless obedience and also by being punished for our sins. In Jesus, God reveals His highest form of greatness. This is expressed in the ultimate sacrifice Jesus made for us by dying for our sins. Start the day remembering that this is the God Who lives in us.

"He was with God in the beginning." We must remember that the One Who lives in us is eternal. This means that He has lived forever. It means that everything that ever happened and ever will happen is before Him right now. He cannot be surprised. We may be surprised at the events of the day, but Jesus, living in us, sees our day perfectly and completely. The One Who lives in us is never surprised!

"Through Him all things were made; without Him nothing was made that has been made." What an overwhelming thought! We are the branches, the body, the building or dwelling place of the Creator of the universe! He is so powerful that merely by speaking all things came to be! Surely if He had enough power to create everything, He has the power to change us for the better. His supernatural life flows into us, starting to grow and change us. We are transformed into His likeness and that glorious process of growth and change will go on forever, for He is eternal and infinite. We can never completely know God.

"In Him was life and the life was the light of men." He is life and light! He is the author of all life—the life of the acorn that changes through growth into the oak tree. He is the author of the life in a grain of rice, which if planted and transplanted will grow into a stalk of rice producing hundreds of new grains. He is the light that causes life to grow and change. Where is He? He lives in us and we are to remain in Him by focusing our minds on Him. In I John 3:2 this mystery is summed up this way. *"Dear friends, now we are children of God, and what we will be has not yet been made known. But we know that when He appears, we shall be like Him, for we shall see Him as He is."*

Learn it:
1. What are the five descriptions of Jesus found in John 1:1–4?
2. What are the "I am" descriptions Jesus gave Himself as recorded in:
   a. John 9:4
   b. John 15:1
   c. John 11:25
   d. John 10:7
   e. John 6:35
3. Are these descriptions easy to use to remind you of Who is in you?

4. Why is reminding ourselves each morning of Who Jesus is so important?
5. What are other Scripture passages to remind ourselves of how great Jesus is?

Do it:
When people looked at his face they turned away. He was scarred badly in a war. He prayed and prayed that God would heal him so that people would no longer shun him. God answered that prayer not by giving healing but by giving him a great ministry of encouragement. This person however, developed a tremendous self-image and carried on an incredible ministry. He traveled the nation, speaking for tens of thousands of people. How did he develop a good self-image in spite of his deformity?

Prayer: Grant, dear Savior, that we may never forget Who You are. May we grow constantly in the realization of Your majesty and Your greatness. Overwhelm us with Your Love. May we marvel that You are the Way to God. May we know today that You will not be surprised by anything in our life, for You see it all. Lord, change us. Grow us into Your image. For Your sake we pray, Amen.

* * * * *

Day Four:
"What do You want today, Jesus?"
"I want you to let My light shine by bearing much fruit."

"I am the vine; you are the branches.
If a man remains in me and I in him
he will bear much fruit." John 15:5

Giving is fruit bearing. Jesus tells us, "*If you remain in me and my words remain in you, ask whatever you wish, and it will be given you. This is to my Father's glory, that you bear much fruit, showing yourselves to be my disciples*" (*John 15:7–8*). This is an amazing promise. Remaining in Christ is to think about Christ, not ourselves. It is to desire the things that Christ desires for us. When our desires match Christ's His life flows into us. When we long to be like Him, to look like Him, to reveal Him through our lives, to let His light shine through us, then He remains in us. These are the fruits of which He speaks. God is the ultimate example of giving. He created life as an example of giving. Trees bear fruit to give it away! They don't keep the fruit for themselves. Life means giving and when Christ comes into us His life and light in us is expressed in the production of spiritual fruit, which is various forms of giving to God and others.

The condition for fruit bearing is cleansing from sin. Fruit bearing starts with cleansing us from sin. To want what Christ wants is to want to be rid of sin. Sin is darkness but Christ is light. When Jesus, as the light of the world (John 9:5), lives in us, His light is to shine in and out of every room of our "house." Imagine that we are like a big house with rooms for different activities. We have a room in which we sleep; a room in which we eat; a kitchen; a room in which we sit and talk with one another. We want the light of Jesus to shine in every room in our house. We don't want Jesus to live in just some parts of our lives. We want Jesus to shine in every part of our life so that we can be like the picture of the house with light shining out everywhere.

King David said it like this. *"Search me, O God, and know my heart; test me and know my anxious thoughts. See if there is any offensive way in me, and*

lead me in the way everlasting" (Psalm 139:23–24).
Our first and deepest longing when Christ comes
into us must be the longing to be made clean. We
want Him to search every room, every area of our
lives. Remember the function of light? Light
destroys darkness! And when we invite Jesus into
every area of our life, His light will destroy darkness.

**The motivation for fruit bearing comes
when Christ fills us.**

Light fills us and changes us from concern for
self to concern for Christ and others. The heart of
sin is selfishness. The light of Christ is selfless sacrifice. The sin of our first representative Adam
was to put his desires before God's desires. God
commanded him not to eat of the Tree of the
Knowledge of Good and Evil, but Adam put
God's command second to his desire for the forbidden fruit. Adam was controlled by selfishness,
not by love for God. What he wanted to do, he
did! When Christ comes into us He fills us to
such an extent that we know we cannot get anything more! We are filled to over flowing and
hence freed from self-concern. He fills us in such
a way that torrents of living water stream from
us (John 7:38). When we remind ourselves that
Christ is in us, and that He is everything, we are
free to give.

**The power for fruit bearing is Christ's life
in us.** We can struggle all we want with selfishness
but if we fail to remember Christ is in us, we will

never conquer it. Only by "remaining in Christ" through focusing our minds on Him will His power flow through us. Only Christ can fill us so full that we get to the point of overflowing. We don't "need to get" any more since Christ has filled us. Paul wrote, *And my God will meet all your needs according to his glorious riches in Christ Jesus"* (Philippians 4:19) The power of His life will transform us. He will enable us to gradually overcome our selfishness. The acorn and the oak tree illustrate the power of growth and life. Remember that growth is a gradual process, it is not instant. There may be relapses. But Christ's life is at work in us, changing us and transforming us from selfishness to selflessness.

The purpose of our life becomes fruit bearing. Not only do we need a new sense of value and a new self-image but we need a new purpose for living. The purpose of living is illustrated in Charles Dickens' story, "A Christmas Carol." Scrooge was a miserable, tight, stingy old man. All he thought about was himself. All he wanted was to get more money. He did not care how many people he hurt. But he was transformed when he saw the joy of giving, and as the story ends Scrooge is dancing through the village. He found a new, satisfying purpose in life—the purpose of fruit bearing. A tree doesn't bear fruit in order to keep it. It bears fruit in order to give it away! In sharing his wealth with others he found the happiness he thought he could have, but never had, in gaining all the money.

Overcoming concern for ourselves allows the light within us to shine out to others in concern for them. Because we have a new sense of self-worth, and a new self-image based on the beauty and power of Christ, we are set free from the demand to constantly get things for ourselves. We are full. Christ is in us. We can give and in that giving allow the light to shine from us. We are transformed to forgive and to give. Because the Savior has filled our needs, we are freed to see the needs of others. It is only when Christ fills us that we can be set free from the constant pity party of feeling so empty and so worthless. When we realize that the "glorious riches of Christ" dwell in us through His presence, we do not have to "get and get" any longer!

Learn it:
1. What is the nature of fruit bearing? (Why do trees bear fruit—to keep it or to give it away?)
2. What is the condition for fruit bearing? Explain why.
3. Can we have sin in us and at the same time have Jesus in us? How does Psalm 139:23–24 answer this?
4. What is the motivation for fruit bearing?
5. What is the power for fruit bearing?

6. How does Ephesians 2:8–10 (especially verse 10) describe our new purpose in life?

Do it:
What steps are necessary in order to allow Christ to cleanse us from our sin?

Prayer: Precious Savior, may we always remain in You so that we may grow and change into Your likeness. Grant that as we grow, rich spiritual fruit may be born in our lives. In Your name we pray, Amen.

* * * * *

Day Five:
"What do You want today, Jesus?"
"I want you to remember that apart from Me you can do nothing."

"I am the vine; you are the branches.
If a man remains in Me and I in him, He
will bear much fruit; *Apart from Me you
can do nothing.*" John 15:5

One of the great stories illustrating the way Jesus works is the story of the feeding of thousands with five little loaves of bread and two fish. This story is found in John 6:5–13. Jesus was in the middle of a great crowd of people estimated at about five thousand men. This meant that there were probably about twenty thousand people, counting the women and children. Jesus was concerned about feeding all these people and so He asked His disciples, "Where shall we buy bread for these people to eat?" (John 6:5). Jesus knew what He was going to do and asked this question only to test the disciples to find out if they would try to solve the problem on their own, or would look to Him to solve it.

The disciples failed the test. One of them said, "Eight months' wages would not be enough to buy all these people food" (John 6:7). They scouted through the crowd and all they could find was a little boy who had five loaves of bread and two fish. They brought it to Jesus, not believing that He could do anything with it.

Jesus told the people to sit down. He took the loaves and fish, prayed to His Father, giving thanks for the food, and then distributed the food to the crowd. Everyone took as much as they wanted. After they had eaten He told His disciples to gather up everything that was left, and the disciples filled twelve large baskets with the pieces of bread and fish that were left.

In this story Jesus illustrates a double truth. The first truth is that apart from Him we can do nothing at all. The second truth is that when we look to Him and trust Him to work through us, amazing things happen. Paul described this when he said, *"Now unto Him Who is able to do exceedingly, abundantly, above all we can ask or imagine"* (Ephesians 3:20). This text describes how Jesus will work when we remain in Him and He remains in us. We must live each day in the three-fold transforming prayer:

- Where are you, Jesus?
- Who are you, Jesus?
- What do you want to do today, Jesus?

Amazing, transforming, inexplicable things will happen which are beyond our wildest dreams and imaginations. If, however, we think of Jesus as being outside of us and we must work for Him in our own power and strength, we will soon find out that we can do nothing.

It is absolutely essential that we learn to build our self-image not on our own power and looks but on the One Who lives in us. When we look to Him to transform us we are looking to the One Who fed thousands of people with five loaves of bread and two fish! When we try to change ourselves it amounts to nothing at all. Each day Jesus tests us as He tested the disciples. He is constantly asking us how we are going to meet the great challenges in our lives. When we pray the three-part "New You" prayer each day, we will always meet every challenge in the One Who lives in us! The apostle Paul understood this when he wrote, *"I can do everything through Him Who gives me strength"* (Philippians 4:13). Do you believe this?

Learn it:
1. What test did Jesus set before His disciples in John 6:7?
2. How did the disciples fail the test? How did they pass the test?
3. How did this miracle illustrate Ephesians 3:20?
4. What is the danger of living by "common sense"?

Do it:
One of the great themes of the New Age Movement is, "What the mind can conceive, man can achieve." How does this lesson prove that statement false? How is that statement limiting according to Ephesians 3:20?

Hartford, Connecticut, is known as a very hard area to reach with the gospel. Virtually no churches are growing. Yet several years ago God used a Christian businessman and his wife, who had no seminary or Bible training, to win more people to Christ in one year than all the churches combined. What do you think they did to achieve this amazing success?

Prayer: Precious Savior, we acknowledge that apart from You remaining in us and our remaining in You, we can do nothing. Thank You for the story of the five loaves and the two fish. Thank You for reminding us that when You worked with that little boy, his lunch was changed to feed thousands of people! Help us to have that kind of faith. You can work with us in unusual ways as we trust Your power within us, and constantly remind us of Who You are. For Your sake we pray, Amen.

* * * * *

Day Six:
"What do You want today, Jesus?"
"I want to remind you that if you do not remain in Me, you will be like a withered, dead branch."

"I am the vine; you are the branches.
If a man remains in Me and I in him,
he will bear much fruit.
Apart from Me you can do nothing.
If anyone does not remain in Me, he is like a
branch that is thrown away and withers. . . . "
John 15:5–6

Jesus closes this passage with a stern warning. We must be serious and disciplined about remaining in Him and He remaining in us or we may become like dead branches. Obviously, any branch cut off from the vine will wither and die. No branch separated from the vine can support leaves and fruit on its own. It must be in the vine to grow. *So too, the most important goal of our life*

must be to have Christ in us. He is like air. We cannot live without Him, for He is our life.

Many of us do not understand this simple truth. We try to build our sense of value apart from Christ's presence in us. We go days without thinking of anything but our own failure or success. We become anxious and worried, or proud and giddy with what we have not or have done. But we seldom rejoice during the day in the fact that we are occupied by Jesus. And this is as senseless as a branch saying to the vine, "I don't need you anymore"! To live apart from Christ is death. It is something like a deep sea diver saying that he doesn't need the air tanks any longer. It is like someone saying, "I don't need to eat any longer. I can do just as well without any food." That person eventually starves to death.

The reason for depression and sadness is the emptiness and the spiritual hunger that we all feel when we refuse to recognize Jesus living in us through His Holy Spirit. We are frustrated because we cannot change ourselves. We feel weak and worthless and that robs us of vision and courage. We are afraid and anxious about the future. All of these are signs of having been cut off from the vine, Jesus Christ. We gradually die without His life flowing into us. To have Jesus in us, and to live His life, will result in excitement, amazement, and constant change for good.

Thus, the power to change ourselves is far more important than we realize. The power to change us is life itself. Christ's life, flowing into us is that which gives us value. Christ's life in us is that which illuminates us and radiates from us giving us beauty that attracts others to Him. Christ's life within us ensures that we shall live forever, for it is eternal life. *"For God so loved the world that whoever believes in Him should not perish but have eternal life"* (John 3:16).

Learn it:
1. Why do we all have feelings of worthlessness at times?
2. Explain the "Where, Who, and What" prayer. What are the parts and why does it work?
3. How important is it to remain in Christ and have Christ remain in us? (Give at least the two reasons from your memory text, but more if you can.)

Do it:
A young Christian businessman was very successful, making over one hundred million dollars in fifteen years. Then he made a bad investment and lost most of his money. Years later, he said that the best years of his life were not when he was successful, but when he was a failure. Can you explain why someone would say this?

Prayer: Precious Savior, grant that we may never be cut off from You. Forgive us for living our lives as if You did not exist. May we daily be conscious of Your presence. May we always remind ourselves that You are in us and You are the greatest Being in the universe. May we always look to You to do that which is beyond our dreams and imaginations. By abiding in You, grant that we may bear rich fruit. In Your name we pray, Jesus. Amen.

* * * * *

Day Seven: Reflection

1. What did you like about the study this week?
2. Was there anything that you did not like or did not understand?
3. What unique new lessons did you learn about God?
4. Did this lesson help you in any practical way? Explain how.

Week Five

"Our New Power to Pray"

"Our Father in heaven, Hallowed be Your name, Your kingdom come, Your will be done on earth as it is in heaven. Give us this day our daily bread; And forgive us our sins as we forgive those who sin against us; and lead us not into temptation but deliver us from evil; For Yours is the kingdom, the power and the glory forever, Amen."
Matthew 6:9–13

Day One: Introduction

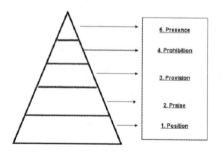

The power to remain in Christ: The great power we receive when Christ dwells in us, after the power to forgive and grow, is the power of prayer. Each time we pray, God promises to answer. This means that He will do something that He would not have done if we had not prayed.

The key to remaining in Christ is to understand and experience all the dimensions of prayer. Many think of prayer primarily as talking to God. They do not realize that there are many dimensions to prayer.

The Lord's Prayer: This week we will be studying the prayer our Lord gave us. In this prayer, commonly known as the Lord's Prayer, we find five parts of prayer which can be illustrated as follows. We can diagram these parts as the "pyramid" of prayer.

- The position of prayer is childlike trust when we begin by addressing God as our Father. This trust is "wordless." Children trust parents without having to say anything.
- Praise forms the second part of prayer as we long for the hallowing of God's name, the coming of His kingdom, and the doing of His will.
- Provision occurs when we ask God our Father to supply all our daily material needs.
- Prohibition starts when we ask God's forgiveness and in that forgiveness forgive

others. It moves beyond this. We pray to be victorious in spiritual battles over demonic forces. We long for deliverance from the evil one.

- The prayer ends with a longing that Christ's presence be established over all the earth as we claim that His is the kingdom, power, and glory forever.

Learn it:

1. What are the five parts of the "pyramid" of prayer"?
2. How do these five parts relate to the five divisions of the Lord's Prayer as those divisions are suggested above?

Do it:

Sam wondered why his prayer time seemed so boring and empty. Often, after he prayed he felt more depressed than before. How can the "pyramid of prayer" help Sam make his prayer life continuous and exciting?

* * * * *

Day Two: "The Position of Prayer"

"Our Father in heaven . . ." Matthew 6:9

The Position of Prayer: Many people do not realize that there is a sign on heaven's door saying, "Only children admitted here!" Jesus said, *"I tell you the truth, unless you change and become like little children, you will never enter the kingdom of heaven. Therefore, whoever humbles himself like this child is the greatest in the kingdom of heaven"* (Matthew 18:3–4).

Children are dependent creatures. They cannot care for themselves. They need parents to protect them, feed them, clothe them, provide them with housing, and train them to grow up. While never taught dependency, children know this. They become very frightened when they are out of the presence of their loving and caring parents.

Adults, however, are often dependent upon themselves and it is hard for them to depend on Jesus like a little child. Jesus said that we must change from adult self-dependency to childlike trust, depending on Him. Only those who like little children trust in Jesus will enter heaven.

Jesus said that we are to have a childlike trust. We are to be blissfully happy trusting that He will protect and provide for us. This is the "position" of prayer. It is the foundation of prayer on which all other forms of prayer rest.

In 1 Thessalonians 5:16–18 Paul tells us to "Be joyful always; **pray continually**; give thanks in all circumstances." If prayer is limited to asking God for things it is impossible to pray continually, for we would never be able to do anything else! We would be talking to God all the time! There is more to prayer than talking. Prayer is an attitude of childlike trust. *It is a childlike relationship of trust.* We can trust always, throughout every day. Dependency is an attitude just as being joyful and being grateful are attitudes. I don't always have to say, "I'm so happy!" to be happy all the time, nor do I have to constantly say "Thank you" in order to have a grateful heart. So too, I don't always have to have my eyes closed and be talking to God to be in prayer. Prayer is being like a little child, filled with joy, gratitude, and quiet, careful trust that loving parents will supply all needs. Most of the time children are not even aware of their trust in their parents. It is natural.

- **An instinct to help . . .** Childlike dependence on Jesus will make us act instinctively to help others. Adults often measure the cost of helping others, while children do not wait but act instinctively and immediately. When we see people in need we will naturally and immediately respond to the Holy Spirit's inner prompting to help that person, just as a little child. This is one of the most important and powerful forms of "wordless" prayer. It is God's Holy Spirit moving within us.

- **An impulse to act . . .** A more direct way of hearing God than acting instinctively is to receive a distinct thought. Sometimes we will be awakened in the night with a special burden for a friend. Sometimes we will have an urge to call someone. We must listen to the Lord and act on these thoughts. Before we begin any major project we should wait in prayer, asking God to show us His plan rather than asking Him to bless ours. One of the greatest positions to be in is the position of not knowing what to do! It gives you the opportunity to be free from your own plans and wait until God clearly opens up the door. While instinct is "wordless" prayer, these sudden thoughts are God directly speaking to us, to act in love for others.

- **Instructions for the moment . . .** There is another way of listening as a little child. Jesus guides us to Scripture verses that give comfort, strength, or guidance for the specific need of the moment. As these verses come into our mind we know that Jesus is speaking to us.

In order to listen to our Savior direct us through His Holy Spirit we must develop the joyful, grateful attitude of a trusting child. This is the foundation, the position of prayer. This is what it means to pray without ceasing—to always be in the attitude of carefree, childlike trust in Jesus.

Learn it:
1. What sign is over heaven's door (Matthew 18:3)?
2. D_____ is the primary characteristic of a child.
3. When we cultivate childlike D_____ we are in the P_____ of prayer.
4. We can pray without words just as we can be J_____ and G_____ without words (1 Thessalonians 5:16–18).

5. Describe what it means to be in the position of prayer, or to pray without ceasing.

6. When we are in the position of prayer we are in a good position to hear God speak to us. What are three of the many ways God speaks to us:

   1. _____
   2. _____
   3. _____

Do it:

Jane awakened at 3:00 a.m., disturbed and troubled. She had a sudden picture (or dream) of a friend who was in serious trouble. What was happening to Jane and how should she react? Do you think we can be in prayer when we are sound asleep? Explain.

Jim received disturbing news that he had cancer. He did not know what to do, so he opened his Bible randomly and asked God to show him some verse of comfort. Was this a good thing to do, or should he have selected some verses that he knew? Defend both positions.

Prayer: Give us that childlike joy and gratitude that comes from carefree trusting in You, Jesus. How we praise You that You care for us so much that You have counted the number of hairs on our head and are concerned when so much as one of them falls out. May we go through each day in this quiet confidence and trust in You. In Your name we pray, Amen.

* * * * *

Day Three: "Praise"

"Our Father in heaven. Hallowed be Your name; Your kingdom come; Your will be done on earth as it is in heaven." Matthew 6:9–10

The necessity of praise: When we are in a position of childlike trust and its resulting carefree, joy-filled, grateful spirit, we will move into the second dimension of prayer, which we call praise. Praise in prayer is as necessary as a wick to a firecracker or in a candle. Unless the wick is lit the candle will not burn and give light nor will the firecracker explode. Unless prayers are filled with praise they will not ascend.

I have prayed many times only to become more discouraged than I was before I began. I could never understand why, until one day I realized that when I prayed I was concentrating only on my problems and not on my Savior. I was mentally reviewing all the difficulties I was facing and was consequently feeling sorry for myself and becoming overwhelmed with the fact that I could not solve my problems. Because I did not see any solution for my problems, I didn't think God could either. My prayers lacked the lifting fire praise.

We cannot maintain a friendship without expressing love and appreciation to each other. If one friend cannot get beyond self-pity to appreciate the other friend, the friendship becomes selfish and destructive. We need to give to each other. Each person must express concern, appreciation, and love for the other. This is the essence of praise. Prayer is not merely expressing our concerns for ourselves, but it is also expressing our concern for God.

Jesus taught us to be polite in praying when He taught us to begin with concern for God and not for ourselves. Concern for God is a form of praise. The opening three petitions of His prayer show concern for the honor of God's name, the coming of His kingdom, and the doing of His will. True praise is concern and appreciation for our Father. Praise is more than thoughts or songs, however. We praise God by our deeds. When we work to hallow God's name, and bring His kingdom, and do His will we are praising God. Praise is more than singing; it is doing God's will.

Hallowed be Your name: This first petition of the prayer deals with the nature and character of God. Names in the Bible describe God. The name "Father," with which Jesus starts this prayer, describes God's caring and providing nature. "Emmanuel" states that God is with us at all times. "Lord, God Almighty", tells us that God is the Lord of all the earth and He is all powerful. The "Good Shepherd" describes Jesus' activity in caring for us.

When we pray that these names be "hallowed" we mean first of all that God be respected. We are saying that we love God so much that we want everyone to love Him. This is the highest form of praise—to not only desire but also do something so that everyone may know Who God is and respect Him by treating all His characteristics with reverence and awe.

Praise extends beyond prayer in words. Praise is offered to God in our deeds as we tell others about this God Whom we have discovered. When we witness we are "hallowing" God's name. When we face persecution because we speak about God we are praising God in very significant and costly ways. Our whole life must be filled with excitement about God; about His love, His purity, His power, His compassion, and His forgiveness in Jesus. It must show in worship, in singing, and in our entire life. One poet put it this way: "May my whole being and my ways, in every part, be filled with praise."

Your kingdom come: Jesus came to establish His Father's rule over the world. Our Father's kingdom is one where everyone is equal. All will be treated justly and with love. It is a kingdom in which there will never be any lying or stealing. People will not hurt each other or hate God. Satan and all the devils will be completely destroyed. Sickness and death will be no more. Sadness and sorrow will be gone and there will be eternal joy. Excitement about this kingdom and working for its establishment are forms of praise, lifting up petitions.

Your will be done on earth as it is in heaven: The beauty of heaven lies in the fact that there is only "one will" in heaven and everyone agrees on it. No one quarrels or argues in heaven for there is nothing to quarrel about. Everyone is agreed—our Father's will is the best! The will of our Father is to give generously and love all. When everyone agrees that our Father's will is best heaven will be achieved. To live this way is to live in praise to God and thus to live in constant prayer.

When we bring our petitions to God we must constantly be praising Him, especially in the three areas of His names, His kingdom, and His will. Without praise and concern for these three areas, our prayers will be ineffective. Hence the foundation of prayer lies in childlike trust in God that leads to concern for our Father's name, kingdom, and will, which is the highest form of praise.

Learn it:

1. How can we show courtesy and politeness when we begin a conversation?
2. The first three petitions of the Lord's Prayer express our courtesy by being concerned about:

   God's N_____

   God's K_____

   God's W_____
3. What is the function of God's names?
4. What does it mean to hallow God's name?
5. What are we praying for when we pray for the coming of God's kingdom?
6. What is the "will" of God?

Do it:

Jim was excited about worship. He joined the people who danced and sang in worship. He shared their joy. However, during the week Jim allowed people to swear in his presence without rebuking them. In his business he paid the lowest wages he possibly could. At home he continuously quarreled and fought with anyone who disagreed with him. He did not show his excitement about God.

a. What form of praise is most important according to I Samuel 15:22: words or conduct?
b. How are our daily lives to be "living praise" to the Lord?

Christ, the light of the world, dwells in us. His purpose in coming was to reveal the beauty and goodness of God.

a. What are some specific, practical ways in which His light in us, shines out of us, and shows God's goodness?
b. What is "praise" according to your answer?

Prayer: Precious Savior, grant that every part of our lives might be filled with praise. Grant that our childlike trust and carefree attitude may give rise to constant praise. May we never be so concerned about ourselves that we fail to be concerned about the hallowing of Your name and the coming of Your kingdom and the doing of Your will. For Jesus' sake we pray, Amen.

* * * * *

Day Four: "Provision"

"Our Father in heaven, Hallowed be Your name, Your kingdom come, Your will be done on earth as it is in heaven. *Give us this day our daily bread . . .*" Matthew 6:9–11

Having expressed our concern for our heavenly Father, Jesus now tells us to express our concerns and needs to our Father. We are polite and courteous in our prayer when we begin in concern for our Father. This politeness is a form of praise. We praise God by longing that His characteristics be respected and His kingdom be established and His will be done everywhere.

It is in that context of praise that we now present our needs to Him. Just as a good earthly father is concerned about his children's needs, so much more our perfect heavenly Father is concerned about all our needs. Jesus said, *"Which of you, if his son asks for bread, will give him a stone? Or if he asks for a fish, will give him a snake? If you, then, though you are evil, know how to give good gifts to your children, how much more will your Father in heaven give good gifts to those who ask Him!" (Matthew 7:9–1)1.*

When it comes to earthly needs we have one of two problems: either we think we have supplied those needs through our *own* wealth and effort and don't need our Father, or we have so little that we doubt our Father cares for us. Satan uses both these tools to make us doubt God. We must remember God's promises to fill all our needs. Here are some of those promises.

Philippians 4:19: *"And my God will meet all your needs according to his glorious riches in Christ Jesus."* While this promise is certainly for everyone, it is especially meaningful to those who live in poverty. There are three key thoughts in this verse.

- First, *God* will meet our needs. We must trust Him as a child trusts parents. God is infinitely wealthy. Our Father in heaven not only owns all, but is all powerful. When the kings of Israel trusted God, God always delivered them. God has given two great pictures of deliverance in the Old Testament: first when He parted the Red Sea so the

Israelites could escape the Egyptians and second when He parted the Jordan River, allowing the Israelites to enter the Promised Land.

- The second concept in this verse is the word "needs." God doesn't promise to give us everything we want. Sometimes when God answers our prayers and gives us what we need it is something that we do not *want*. However, He knows we need it desperately in order to prepare us for heaven. It is important to realize that this life is a school preparing us for eternal life and we have many important lessons to learn. Some of these lessons include suffering and hardship as the only way to mature us (James 1:2–4).

- The third concept in this verse is the idea that God's provision for us is measured by "his glorious riches in Christ Jesus." God will provide for our needs far beyond all the limits of our imaginations (Ephesians 3:20).

Matthew 18:19: *"Again, I tell you that if two of you on earth agree about anything you ask for, it will be done for you by my Father in heaven."*

This is a unique promise of provision that is often misunderstood. There is special power in prayer when two or more of us agree on something in prayer. Some object to this, saying that it teaches that we can get God to change His mind if more than one person prays. In other words, God responds to the "pressure" of many praying.

We have fifteen grandchildren. If just one of them asks us to do something, we certainly will listen, but if all fifteen come to us, surround us, hold hands, and ask us as their grandma and grandpa to do something, we will surely give special attention to that. There is a special delight that our Father has when we join hands together in unity and love and as His family members unite together in prayer. This is not extra pressure but is simply a powerful expression of love and unity.

John 15:16,17: *"You did not choose Me, but I chose you . . . to go and bear fruit—fruit that will last. Then the Father will give you whatever you ask in My name. This is My command: love one another."*

In this third verse we see the condition on which our requests for provision will be granted. We can ask for whatever we need in order to bear much fruit and the Father will grant it as long as we ask for it in the name of the One Who lives in us. The fruit that Christ wants us to bear is explained and summarized: love one another. God will give us *anything* we need in order for us to be able to love one another!

Learn it:

1. According to Matthew 7:9-11 how can we be absolutely certain that our Father in heaven will meet all our needs?

2. According to Philippians 4:19 to what "extent" will God meet our needs? Explain the meaning of this phrase.

3. Why does God take special delight when two or more people gather for prayer? Are these prayers more "effective" than the prayers of a single person? What is different about them?

4. For what reason, according to John 15:16-17, will God answer our prayers?

Do it:

Mary, a single mom, owned her own home, but the mortgage payments were more than she could handle. She became desperate and put her home up for sale. She prayed and prayed that the house would sell, but it did not. Mary struggled more and more with finances and became desperate. She prayed for "daily bread" but it did not seem to come. How would you counsel Mary with what you learned from this lesson?

Explain the difference between what we want and what we need. Give examples of how what we want can be pleasant at first but painful in the long run. Give examples of how what we need can be painful at first but good for us in the long run.

Prayer: Thank you, Savior, for encouraging us to ask our Father to fill all our needs. As You live in us, as You have made us Your branches and body and building, may we have all we need to be instruments of Your love. In Your name we pray, Jesus. Amen.

* * * * *

Day Five: "Prohibition"

"Our Father in heaven, Hallowed be Your name,
Your kingdom come, Your will be done on earth
as it is in heaven. Give us this day our daily bread
*And forgive us our sins as we forgive those who
sin against us. And lead us not into temptation
but deliver us from evil.*" Matthew 6:9–13

Several years ago I was involved in an exhausting
speaking tour. For four weeks I conducted a day-
long seminar, each day in a different city. I would
travel from one city to another at night. I returned
home for weekends, but on the final weekend I
was so exhausted that when I got home I laid
down on the sofa and stared at the ceiling, saying
nothing, until nearly midnight.

Finally my wife knelt beside me and quietly
started to pray. Suddenly I sat bolt upright! I
asked her what she was doing and she replied,
"I was prohibiting Satan and his demons from

bothering you anymore." The change in emotions was one of the most dramatic, sudden, surprising transformations I have ever experienced. The demonic entity that had attacked, sensing my extreme weariness as his opportunity, was prohibited from operating anymore by my wife's prayer. This spirit recognized the authority of Jesus, Who lives in my wife. As that spirit was bound, I went from the depths of weariness to the heights of praise.

We had another similar experience a few years later. I left for work one morning in deep depression. Throughout the day, the depression mysteriously left. When I returned home that evening I walked up to the house whistling and singing, something I rarely do. My wife greeted me at the door with a big smile, and I asked her what she had done during the day. She told me that she had spent the day fasting and praying that the "evil one" would leave me alone. Once again, she had prohibited demonic spirits from attacking using the authority and power of the One Who lives in her. The change in my condition was nothing short of supernatural. In both these instances she was acting as part of God's police force. In the authority of Christ, clothed with the uniform of prayer, she was "arresting" evil spirits.

As disciples of Jesus we must be aware of two things. First, Satan and his demons are constantly watching and waiting for times to attack us with temptation. Second, Jesus teaches us to pray, after having been forgiven, that we not only be spared these attacks but also, if they do come, that we prohibit or forbid the demonic powers to conquer us. It is most appropriate to pray for deliverance from the "evil one" and his legions. Jesus Himself taught us to do this. In Luke 9:1 we are told, *"When Jesus had called the Twelve together, he gave them power and authority to drive out all demons."*

We have included "prohibition" as one of the levels or phases of prayer. This is the activity of prohibiting the activity of the evil one in our lives through the presence and authority of Christ Who lives in us.

The meaning of "lead us not into temptation": There are various situations in life in which we are especially vulnerable to demonic attack. While it is a blessing to go through them victoriously, it is not wrong to ask our heavenly Father, for Jesus' sake, to excuse us from them. And, when we are in them we are to wear the uniform of Christ's police force—the uniform of prayer. He is in charge of our lives and He leads us. At times, as He did with His own Son, He will allow us to enter a battlefield with demonic power. This is called temptation. *"Then Jesus was led by the Spirit into the desert to be tempted by the devil"* *(Matthew 4:1)* Jesus was led, by the Holy Spirit, into battle with Satan. It was an agonizing time.

It was so exhausting for our Lord that at the end *"angels came and attended him"* (Matthew 4:11). We too, from time to time, will be tested. These are exhausting battles. Paul tells us that we wrestle not with flesh and blood but with principalities and powers (Ephesians 6:12).

Here are some examples of our spiritual battlegrounds.

- **Poverty:** The constant, wearisome, daily grind of not having enough money or food is a favorite opportunity for demonic powers to lead us into the sin of bitterness, or other sins such as stealing or selling our bodies in order to get enough food. Jesus teaches us to plead, for His sake, that we be delivered from poverty. He also gives us authority to prohibit the demonic powers from afflicting us when we are poor, by binding them in His name (Matthew 18:18). Jesus also teaches that the way out of poverty is to tithe! (Malachi 3:10).
- **Persecution:** While persecution may be necessary for revitalizing the disciples of Jesus, it also can be very dangerous. God is using persecution in India to light fires of revival, but at the same time there are casualties in this spiritual battle. Some will fall away from following the Savior. Demonic power can be very active in times of persecution. It is right to pray for freedom from persecution. But we must also prohibit the evil

spirits from working in times of persecution by praying for deliverance from them.

- **Pain:** Chronic illness, disability, and continuous pain are also opportunities both for tremendous experience of God's power but also for discouragement and lack of faith. Paul pleaded with God to take away his mysterious disability, but God refused (2 Corinthians 12:9). Paul had to live on this battlefield for many years.

- **Prosperity:** Perhaps the most dangerous battleground, the one in which demonic powers are most successful, is material prosperity. When we become wealthy we tend to trust our money and talents rather than God and we can wander very far from Him.

The meaning of "deliver us from the evil one": Many of the newer translations eliminate the word "one" and render this as "deliver us from evil." However there is ample reason to use "evil *one*" also. When Christ dwells within us, He brings into our being His authority over the "evil ones" or demonic spirits. He gives us the right to invoke this authority by rebuking them in His name. Deliverance from evil, from the "evil one" and "evil ones" is based on Colossians 2:15. *"And having disarmed the powers and authorities [evil ones], he made a public spectacle of them, triumphing over them by the cross."* Our Lord has disarmed and humiliated the demonic hosts. Christians who do not use the power and authority of the One Who lives in them in their spiritual battle with evil, open themselves to incredible attacks and crippling spiritual weakness.

Our urban areas are wracked with problems of inner-city slums. Violence, child abuse, gangs, sexual crimes abound. And yet cities are also filled with Christians. But these Christians do not understand that since Christ lives in them they are now God's police force, given Christ's authority to rebuke demonic powers, arrest them, and demolish the strongholds of lies which they create. As the Good News sweeps through developing countries, the new Christians are far more aware of their value and power in Christ than Western Christians seem to be. During the twentieth century disciples in the developing countries, including India, made more disciples than the total number made in the previous nineteen hundred years!

Prayer begins with childlike trust and moves into childlike praise and adoration for our Father in heaven. It continues with a simple trust that all our needs will be met and the measure by which they are met is the "riches of Christ Jesus." The fourth dimension in prayer deals not only with the forgiveness of our sins and our ability to forgive those who have sinned against us, but also with the authority and power of Christ, Who lives in us, to prohibit demonic activity in our lives. As we realize Who lives in us, we will grow in exercising His authority and power against the demonic spirits which constantly attempt to lead us into sin.

Learn it:
1. How do you explain Ephesians 6:12?
2. Do you believe that demons attack Christians? Can you give any illustrations?
3. What are some common battlefields in which we wage war with demonic powers? Give some additional examples to those given in the lesson.
4. Why does God allow this spiritual warfare to go on (James 1:1–4)?
5. Who is Christ according to Colossians 2:15?
6. Since this Christ is in us, what does this mean for us when we engage in spiritual warfare?
7. Is it permissible to pray for escape from spiritual warfare? Answer this in the light of 1 Corinthians 10:13.

Do it:
No matter what Sam did it was not right. His boss constantly found fault and shouted at him. He was even beaten at times. He found it more and more difficult to take the treatment and could not control his growing rage and resentment. He would dream of ways to embarrass this person

and eventually get even with him. In the light of what you have learned about Christ being in you, what advice would you give Sam?

Prayer: Savior, forgive us for failing to use Your power to rebuke the evil one. Lord, we have unnecessarily allowed the evil one entrance into our lives. Holy Spirit, empower us to prohibit the presence of these evil spirits and thus enable us to live more victoriously. In Your name, Jesus, we pray.

* * * * *

Day Six: "Presence"

"Our Father in heaven, Hallowed be Your name, Your kingdom come, Your will be done on earth as it is in heaven. Give us this day our daily bread; and forgive us our sins as we forgive those who sin against us. And lead us not into temptation but deliver us from the evil one. For Yours is the kingdom, the power and the glory forever, Amen." Matthew 6:9–15

"Again, I tell you that if two of you on earth agree about anything you ask for, it will be done for you by My Father in heaven. For where two or three come together in my name, there I am with them" (Matthew 18:19–20).

I took a number of American pastors into a Hindu temple in India. It was the first time any of them had visited a temple, and they were shaken by the short tour. All of them were burdened and depressed as we left. On the bus ride back to Chennai they shared their experiences. As they were talking I noticed a small village along the road ahead. I asked if they would like to stop and walk through it. They all agreed, so we stopped the bus, got out, and walked into the village. As we entered the village I told them that I could sense the presence of Christ in the village. Since I had never been in the village they were a little skeptical and asked how I could tell. One of the physical signs was neatness and cleanliness, but there also seemed to be a soft, spiritual atmosphere. We heard singing as we walked into the village. Hidden at the back of the village we found a Church of South India and a Christian school. Boys and girls were singing familiar hymns. The contrast in the "feelings" we had in the temple and in the village were amazing.

Christ blesses geographic areas with His presence when two or more gather to worship and pray. Some close friends began work in a government housing project which was riddled with violence and averaged about fifteen police calls per day. Some "old ladies" from a neighboring church wanted to know how they could help. They told them to pray for the project. They took the challenge seriously, and once a week gathered in their church, directing their prayers for an hour to the project. God answered so dramatically that within that year the number of police calls dropped from fifteen a day to about fifteen that year.

God blesses geographic areas, like slums and specific villages and even temple areas, when we claim them for Him through prayer. God will bless houses, shops, factories, school buildings, and even entire states when two or more people are meeting to pray for the area. Normally when coming to Kolkata, India, I experience heavy spiritual oppression. One day was an exception. Arriving in the airport, I felt light hearted and full of praise. After some time, I awakened to the fact that on this particular day millions of people, around the world, were praying for this specific city. I could feel the presence of Christ in a new way.

The Lord's Prayer ends with a doxology, "For Yours is the kingdom, power, and glory, forever." While it may be doubtful that Jesus actually included this hymn of praise in His prayer (that's why you won't find it in most of Bible translations) it is commonly accepted that He expected this hymn to be added since it was the custom of His day and since it is a marvelous summary of the prayer.

It is the claim that Christ makes that everything, every place, and every person belong to Him. As we gather in family devotions, in small prayer cells, and in group worship, we must claim the physical areas in which we meet for Jesus so that the kingdom, power, and glory of Jesus may be shown in them. Jesus promises that where two or three are gathered in His name, there He will be. I believe that He blesses all within that geographic area with His presence because of those who are praying. Let us pray Christ's presence, His kingdom, power, and glory, into our fields, shops, schools, neighborhoods, villages, cities, states, and nations!

Learn it:
Share experiences you have had both with the feeling of the presence of a good and peaceful spirit in a place, and with a frightening, dark demonic spirit.

Do it:
For several weeks, three girls met once a week for prayer in a very violent, troubled neighborhood. Drug dealers used the house next door to peddle drugs. Strange things started to happen on the street, but the strangest occurred one night as the girls were praying. Suddenly, one of them stopped the prayers and said they had to go next door to meet the drug dealers. They all agreed, and went next door to tell the dealers that they had been praying for them. Much to their amazement these violent men were willing to listen, and then gave their lives to Christ.

Prayer: Precious Savior, hear our prayers. Fill not only this room, but our entire neighborhoods, our schools, our places of work, houses, and stores with Your peaceful presence. In Your name we pray. Amen.

* * * * *

Day Seven: Reflection

1. What did you like about the study this week?
2. Was there anything that you did not like or did not understand?
3. What unique new lessons did you learn about God?
4. Did this lesson help you in any practical way? Explain how.

Week Six

"Our New Power to Give Life"

"He who believes in Me, as the scripture says from within him will flow rivers of living water. By this He meant the Spirit, whom those who believed in Him were later to receive." John 7:38, 39 (Henriksen)

Day One: Introduction

Ezekiel 47:1–12: How valuable is a person who has the ability to "give life"? How important is such a person? These are important questions for all believers. When Jesus lives in us He transforms us to be "life-givers." He tells us in our verse for this week that whoever believes in Him will become the headwaters, or the origin of rivers, of living water. Living water is life-giving water. Multiple rivers will flow from us. We are not to be "occasional" life-givers but life is to gush out of us like water in swollen streams after the rain.

When Jesus spoke these astounding words, He was standing in the temple during the highest celebration of the Jewish year. The people were celebrating a vision of the prophet Ezekiel, which is recorded in Ezekiel 47:1–12. Ezekiel saw a trickle of water flowing from the temple, which was located on a hill about 13 kilometers above the Dead Sea. The Dead Sea is one of the saltiest seas in the world, so salty that no life exists in it or around it.

An angel showed Ezekiel how that little trickle of water expanded into a mighty river. He measured the stream four times. First, the stream was only up to his ankles in depth; then it rose to his knees; then to his waist; and finally it was too deep to cross. The water gushed down the slope into the Dead Sea and as it hit the Dead Sea swarms of fish appeared. The water brought life into the sea! Ezekiel turned around and looked back up the stream and saw that the barren land all around the sea had been transformed with fruit trees which bore a crop every month!

John 7:37–39: The Jews believed that this was a picture of God dwelling in their nation, specifically in the temple in Jerusalem. From His dwelling, blessings would flow out to the world. Every year they re-enacted this vision. The priests, wearing white robes with golden sashes, went down to a pool to fill golden pitchers with the water. Then, with great ceremony, they entered the courtyard of the temple and poured out the water on the floor so that it flowed out of the temple.

It was during this enactment of the vision that Jesus stood up, and shouted so that He was heard above the noise of the crowd, "HE WHO BELIEVES IN ME, FROM WITHIN HIM WILL COME RIVERS OF LIVING WATER!" (John 7:37–39). One can hardly imagine the impact these amazing words had on the Jews celebrating this vision.

Another "self-image" picture: In our final week we will look at another picture of who we become when Jesus comes to live in us. We started this course picturing ourselves as houses radiating light into the darkness. Jesus' light shines from within us, just as the light of a house shines out from that house at night. The Bible has other pictures and symbols explaining the meaning of Christ living in us. In this lesson we will see that when Christ lives in us He transforms us to become *the origin of rivers of living water.* We will see ourselves as eternal life-givers! We will see ourselves as the starting point of His rivers of living water, transforming the Dead Sea of sin to life. Our lives will become streams of water, resulting in persons all around us coming to life and, like fruit trees, bearing fruit continuously.

Learn it:
1. How does this picture illustrate Ezekiel 47?
2. Explain how the Jews acted out this vision in their annual feast.
3. Why were the words Jesus shouted out at the time of the celebration (John 7:37–38) so startling to the crowd?
4. What additional self-image picture will we consider in this final week?

Do it:
How is "living water" flowing from your life? How can you increase the flow?

* * * * *

Day Two: The Origin of the Rivers of Living Water

"He who believes in Me, even as the Scripture says." John 7:38

Who suffered the most? Who has suffered more, God or humans? I will never forget my first impressions of India. I became angry with God when I saw all the poverty, sickness, and despair. I questioned God, asking Him why He didn't do something to help all these suffering people. As I asked the question, God put this question in my mind: "John, I think I have done something. What is it?" The answer came immediately. Of course God has done something and it is something far greater than all people who have ever lived could ever do. He gave His Son to suffer hell for all of us, including the lost of India.

Who has suffered more? Let's put all human suffering together from Adam and Eve, the first people who lived, until today. Sum it all up. Think of all the suffering that the whole human race has endured. Compare that to God's suffering. Who has suffered more?

God has! All the suffering of the human race has been "*temporary*" suffering. God, in Jesus Christ, suffered "*eternal*" punishment for our sins when He died on Calvary's cross. On that cross He uttered the most profound statement ever heard by human ears, "My God, My God, why have You forsaken Me?" (Matthew 27:46). In that moment He finished the *eternal* punishment for our sins. What would take an eternity for each of us, Christ did in a moment. We cannot fully understand it, but we can understand that God's suffering for us is infinitely greater than all the suffering all humans have ever endured, for Jesus bore our *eternal* punishment for sin.

It is finished—God's low point or high point? After crying out "My God why have you forsaken Me?" Jesus uttered a sigh of relief as He said, "It is finished" (John 19:30). This means that the punishment for our sins is completely, fully, and eternally paid for and Jesus can "flow" into us through the presence of His Holy Spirit. People often think of Christ's suffering punishment for our sins as the low point. In a way the low point is actually the high point. We see the true nature of God's love and beauty revealed in the sacrifice of Christ. It is in these pain-filled words that Christ reveals the wonder of infinite love. It is the low point that is God's high point. And it is this low point that releases the new life of Christ to flow into us.

Transformed to become rivers of living water. In order for living water to be released from us we must sacrifice, as Christ did. The moment we sacrifice ourselves we open the flood gates of the water of life to flow from us.

When Paul said, "I was crucified with Christ and I died . . ." he was stating that it was at his point of replacing his desires to exalt himself with the desire to sacrifice himself for Christ and others that living waters began to flow from him. Even as the living waters of life were released through Christ giving His life for us, so they will be released from us only when we start giving our life to others. When Paul said that he was crucified with Christ and he died, he was stating that he had found a new principle of living. He no longer lived to selfishly pursue his own desires. He did not want to exalt himself. He was not trying to climb high up to be known by all people. As painful as it might be, he willingly and joyfully set aside all his own desires in order to do what Christ wanted. Loving Christ, not himself, became his joy. When he loved Christ more than himself, torrents and rivers of living water were released from him.

Whenever we give, as God has given to us, we open ourselves up so that rivers of living water can flow from us. This is life-giving water—water that will nourish and heal. It is water that brings eternal life through God's Word and the power of the Holy Spirit.

As you build a new self-image, add to the picture of the house giving light this great picture of rivers of water flowing from you. See yourself as the "headwaters" or the spring which is the beginning of the river. These rivers of water will flow into areas you have never even thought of reaching.

A young mother had serious cancer. A group of Christian ladies prayed for her healing daily. One day she shared that she had a dream and in that dream she saw great streams of people from India pouring into heaven because of her life. The people praying for her thought she would be healed because God gave her this vision. However, she died a few months later. Five years after her death a man from India came to the church with a tract. The woman who died had written out her testimony and it had found its way to India and was printed as a tract. The little pamphlet had been used to plant four churches in India. Her dream was being fulfilled! Even on her death bed, this young mother had become the origin of rivers of living water.

Learn it:
1. Why can we say that Jesus has suffered infinitely more than the total amount of suffering all humans have endured from creation until today?
2. Explain why Jesus' death on the cross, which seems to be the "low point" of His life and the depth of His suffering, is really the "high point" of God's glorious love. Read Romans 5:6–8.
3. Explain why Christ's death on the cross could release rivers of life-giving water to flow into every nation of the world.
4. Explain why when we live for ourselves we shut off rivers of living water, but when we give ourselves in humble service to others, the rivers of water flow.

Do it:
A young man was badly crippled through an accident and lost the use of his legs. He was not discouraged and set out to prove that crippled people are as valuable as everyone else. He got a wheelchair and organized races for those confined to wheelchairs. He pushed his wheelchair all across his nation and gained much publicity. Government officials noticed and soon funds were being

raised to provide wheelchairs for the poor. Explain how this man's misfortune released rivers of living water.

Prayer: Precious Savior, we rejoice that You have perfectly FINISHED all our punishment. We praise You that through Your pain and suffering You opened the way to live in us and transform us to be Your temples. Grant that as we give ourselves sacrificially to you we may become the origins of rivers of living water. Thank You, Jesus, for making us to be Your life-givers. Show us today where You want the water of life to flow. In Your name we pray, Amen.

* * * * *

Day Three: "The Direction of the Streams"

"He who believes in me, as the scripture say . . .
from within him. . . ." John 7:38

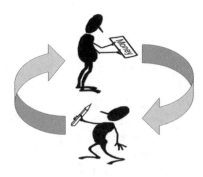

I have a pencil. You want that pencil. I want your money. We agree that you will give me a certain amount of money and we exchange. I give you the pencil, you give me the money. We are both happy. This is called the equal exchange of valuable things.

This equal exchange happens daily all over the world. It happens in the marketplace, in stores, on computers, and between big companies. It is this constant, equal exchange of goods and services that builds relationships.

All relationships are built on mutual exchange: giving and receiving. Loving unions are set up between friends and within marriages when both parties are giving and receiving equally. Persons who merely want to receive, or get things, without giving anything back are like parasites, sucking the life out of a relationship. Criminals want to get (steal) without giving anything back of value.

God's outward flow: The Bible tells us that while there is only one God, He exists as three, equal but distinct Persons, Father, Son, and Holy Spirit. While we cannot *fully* understand this there is an aspect of it that we can understand. These three Persons live in perfect love for each other. They are always giving and receiving and hence they exist in perfect harmony. They are constantly giving to each other—the flow is outward from the Father to the Son and the Spirit. Jesus the Son loves the Father and the Spirit and sacrifices for them. The Spirit flows outward in bringing glory to the Son and the Father. As they give to each other they also then receive from each other. The Triune God is the highest example of giving and receiving. God is the greatest picture of selflessness. The Triune God is a perfect "giving and receiving" relationship. God is always pouring out to others, especially to the smallest and the least of us. God also delights in receiving our love, obedience, and praise. He created us to give and receive with Him.

Satan's inward flow: When God created the angels He made them to be "ministering spirits." In other words they existed to give to Him and to each other as well as receive from God and each other. We do not know how one of them, Satan, got twisted and wanted only to receive or get without ever giving to others. Instead of serving God, he wanted to become God and have all the angels and God serve him. He wanted the highest place so that everyone would give to him. Nothing would come from "within him" to serve others but all others would pour their gifts into him. He changed the direction of the flow from selfless service of others to selfish demands that all others serve him. In a sense, Satan became a "half circle." He cut himself off from all unity and harmony. He could not be with God and the other angels since he had only half of a relationship. Half of any relationship is receiving. The other half is giving. Until the two are joined there can be no loving relationship. His "half circle" of getting only, and not giving, made him unfit for heaven. God excluded him and approximately one-third of the angels who followed him from heaven. These fallen angels became the demons. They are parasites, sucking everything they can and giving nothing in return. All criminals, thieves, robbers, murderers follow in their line. People who are only interested in what they get and not in what they give back of equal value are sinners, or in other words, are parasites sucking life out of all they contact.

Adam's change from outward to inward: When God created Adam He placed him over all His creation so that Adam could give to everything God made. He would give to creation and the created world would give back to him. When God saw that Adam was all alone, He decided to make a partner for him and created Eve. He intended that the two of them would give to each other and receive from each other. Eve was created to give to Adam and Adam was expected to give to Eve. While equal, man and woman are different. Each gives unique gifts to the other and receives unique gifts. In Adam and Eve's giving and receiving a full circle would be set up which would be a loving union, resembling the union the Triune God has within Himself.

God also expected that in return for all He had given to Adam and Eve they would also give back to Him. He created them not only to give and receive with nature and each other, but most of all to give and receive in their relationship with Him. He asked that the gift they give Him would be obedience. He told them not to eat of the Tree of the Knowledge of Good and Evil.

Satan tempted Adam and Eve by telling them that they should GET the fruit of the forbidden tree and forget about giving God anything. He tempted them to believe the "half circle" lie, namely, that all we need to be concerned about is what we get. When people think only about getting, they eventually destroy not only all others around them, but also nature and their relationship with God. "Half circle" people, people who think only of what they can get and never what they can give, are spiritually dead people.

Satan got Adam and Eve to become "half circle" people by getting them to think of how beautiful and delicious the fruit was. He encouraged them to think ONLY of what they were to get, not what God wanted them to give. When they disobeyed God they sinned. This means that they made "getting" the most important thing in their life. No longer did they live to give, or have waters flow from within them out to others. They changed the direction of their life. Now the streams would only flow into them.

A disciple is transformed from getting to giving. When Paul said, "I was crucified with Christ and I died and now Christ lives in me" (Galatians 2:20) he meant that the "inward flow," the selfish grasping, the living to get from others, died. The "half circle" of merely getting was gone. The principle of having everything flow into him died. He now lived on a new principle, the full circle of both giving and receiving. Since Christ lived in him, he could now receive and give to all creation. He was full of Jesus Christ. This fullness gave him infinite resources. The principle of having to constantly get, without giving back something of equal value, was gone. It died. He could now receive and give to God. I want to state it again: a disciple of Jesus can give because he is so full of Christ that he has infinite resources in Jesus, which enable him to give. When Christ lives in us He fills us with Himself. He is without limits. His love has no limit. His power has no limit. His wealth and resources have no limit. Everything we ever want or need we find in the One Who now lives in us. Thus, we can be transformed into the joy of giving. What joy exists when we are both giving and receiving. This is heaven!

Learn it:

1. How is the Triune God, Father Son, and Holy Spirit, the ultimate picture of giving and receiving?

2. What is meant when we say that Satan became a "half circle"?

3. Read Genesis 1 and 2. How did God show the true relationship of giving and receiving in dealing with Adam and Eve? What commands did God give to Adam and Eve so that their direction would be like His?

4. How is conversion a change in the direction of your life?

Do it:

The young man wanted to get as much as he could. It did not matter how he got it. He cheated, lied, and hurt others. He became very wealthy and was very miserable. One day someone told him about Jesus and how the Father in heaven gave His own Son to save us. He gave his life to the Lord and started to show concern for others and started giving his wealth to help the poor. He was startled at the tremendous joy he discovered. Why did the young man suddenly feel "whole" and at peace?

Prayer: Savior, grant that we may rejoice in how much we give. Grant that we may enjoy having the rivers of Your life-giving water flow from within us to bring life to all around us. Free us from being only a "half circle," concerned only about what others give. May we graciously receive and enjoy Your gifts and others' gifts as well. In return may we give back to You and to them. For Your sake we pray. Amen.

* * * * *

Day Four:
"The Miraculous Increase of the Rivers"

"He who believes in Me, as the scripture says, *from within him shall flow rivers.* . . ." John 7:38

A strange increase: Jesus promises that all who believe in Him will have not just one river flowing from them but will have many rivers flowing from within them. In other words, even though we may think our lives to be small and insignificant, God will grant a marvelous increase beyond anything we can imagine.

The vision in Ezekiel shows this mysterious increase. The stream flowing from the temple increases in depth and intensity as Ezekiel measures it. First it is only ankle deep; then it expands to knee deep; and then waist deep; and finally it grows to be too wide to wade through. This is a picture of the life of every believer. When we become origins of rivers of living water, God does things through us that are far beyond our comprehension.

Not only does the stream increase, but the results are abundant. Among the many results are these:

- *"Swarms of living creatures will live wherever the river flows..." (47:9)* In other words, all kinds of animals will live from the effects of the river.
- *"There will be large numbers of fish, because this water flows there"* Where there were no fish, now huge schools of fish swim.
- *"Fishermen will stand along the shore..." (47:10)* The river produces more than life and fish, it blesses the fishermen with abundant catches.
- *"Fruit trees of all kinds will grow on both banks of the river."*
- *"their leaves will not wither..."*
- *"nor will their fruit fail. Every month they will bear."*
- *"their fruit will serve for food..."*
- *"and their leaves for healing."*

Ezekiel mentions eight specific results—abundant results of the rivers of life.

- Swarms of living creatures.
- Abundance of fish
- Food for fishermen
- Fruit trees of all kinds
- Non-dying leaves
- Constant monthly harvests of fruit
- Food from the fruit
- Healing from the leaves

As we reflect on these eight effects God is picturing for us what will happen from our lives when the rivers of living water flow. We cannot imagine all that He will do through us.

It doesn't matter how small you are! I was visiting an orphanage in India where I was introduced to a tiny ten-year-old little girl who had gone to Children's Bible Club and come to believe in Jesus. She wanted to teach the courses to her friends, but her teacher told her she was too young, too little, and besides that, all the workbooks had been used up. The little girl was not hindered, however, since she had memorized all the lessons.

She went out, organized her own clubs, and taught over ninety of her friends the glorious truths about Jesus. Many of these friends were transformed and taught their parents and over fifty adults were also transformed in following Jesus! A church was planted through her testimony. Someone gave Mission India five dollars and God took that trickle and turned it into a mighty river when He used it to provide the course and teacher needed to reach the little orphan girl. The gift then began to multiply in a mysterious way as one disciple after another was reached.

Think of what happened through a little ten-year-old orphan in just one year. Think of all the other children who were transformed. Think of their parents. Think of all the rivers of living water that were flowing through each of these new disciples! Each of the other children and each parent that followed Jesus became a new source of more rivers of living water, all starting from the little girl in just one vacation period!

We never can see what great things God is doing through our lives. When we give gifts of love and service to others, God will multiply those gifts thousands of times over and that multiplication will continue for years and years until Jesus comes again.

God's multiplication: God doesn't use addition, He multiplies our work. When we give one-tenth of all that we make each week to Him, He promises that He in turn will open the "floodgates" of heaven and pour out on us blessings so great that we cannot contain them (Malachi 3:10). Paul tells us that when we "sow generously" or give generously, God in turn will not only give generously to us but will multiply our seed for sowing. The more we give, the more God blesses our resources to give (2 Corinthians 9:10). Perhaps the most wonderful of all promises is found in Ephesians 3:20, where God tells us, **"Now unto Him Who can do immeasurably more than all we can ask or imagine . . ."**

Learn it:
1. Jesus tells us that more than one river will flow from us when we give. Give examples of how this can happen.
2. Not only will the number of rivers increase when we give but also the effects of the rivers will increase. List the eight results of Ezekiel's river as found in the devotional and explain how this could happen from the rivers that flow from your life.
3. How does feeling small and insignificant discourage us from doing anything? How does this vision correct feeling like that?
4. How do each of these verses (Malachi 3:10; 2 Corinthians 9:10; Ephesians 3:20) show that God always multiplies the effects of our giving?

Do it:
Who are some of the people you have helped and how has God multiplied what you did, through their lives?

Prayer: Dear Jesus, fill us to overflowing with the living waters so that rivers of living water may flow from us to others. Show us today some of the ways in which the river coming from us turn into rivers through others so that we might praise You more. In Your name we pray, Amen.

* * * * *

Day Five:
"The Resulting Miracles of Life"

"He who believes in Me, as the scripture says . . . from within him shall flow rivers *of living water . . .*" John 7:38

The leaky bucket: An old Indian water carrier carried two leather buckets from the well to the village many times each day. One leather bucket was new. The other bucket was old, cracked, and leaky. Every morning he faithfully went to the well and filled both and then brought the water back to the village. By the time he got to the village however, the old bucket was only half full since much of the water had leaked out on the way.

One day the old bucket said to the water carrier, "Why do you put up with me? Can't you see that when you get to the village half of the water has leaked out? Why don't you buy another new bucket and save yourself some work?"

The water carrier laughed. "Old bucket, you do not know how I use you every morning, do you? Have you ever noticed all the flowers along your side of the path? I water those flowers every morning with the water which leaks out of you. On the side of the new bucket there are no flowers!"

We often feel like leaky buckets and think that God should trade us in for someone who is more talented and effective. The devil wants us to think that we don't amount to anything. He wants us to think that we are not valuable, that we are ugly and worthless. He tries to convince us every day that we are like that old leaky bucket. God cannot use us because we are not talented enough or don't have enough money.

But just as the water carrier used the leaks in the old bucket to water the flowers along the path, without the bucket knowing it, so God uses our leaks and weaknesses in His own way. We too may not know how God uses us. Through our weaknesses God's power for new life can flow to others. Our weaknesses and frailties help display God's power. When we are so talented, so good, and so powerful that everyone looks up to us, we get in the way of having them see God in us. All they can see are our talents. If they cannot see Jesus in us because they are distracted by our talents, then we cannot be used to bring living water to them. Only when people see Jesus in us will life flow into them, and they can see Jesus best when the only explanation for what we do is that there is some supernatural power at work within us.

Selvi: Selvi was an illiterate mother of four living in a slum in Chennai. She was often cheated at the marketplace because she could not count. Her husband beat her for losing so much money and she slipped into depression and despair.

A group of actors came to her village and performed some skits showing how important it was to learn to read and write and Selvi, with her husband's permission, enrolled in the class. She soon learned how to read and write, but she learned more. She learned about Jesus and Jesus came into her heart.

Rivers of living water began to flow from Selvi's life. First, she saw the importance of getting her children into school. Instead of letting them do nothing she insisted not only that they go to school but that they do their work well. Her children's lives were changed for the better. More importantly, she told them, and her husband, about Jesus and Jesus came to live in all of them. Selvi was transformed to become the origin of "rivers of life." Eternal life came to her husband and her children through her witness!

But it did not stop there. Many in the literacy class noticed how Selvi was changing. Earlier she had merely been sitting around her house all day, in deep depression, concerned only about herself. She did not clean the house. She did not care for her husband's needs or her children's needs. But after Jesus came into her life, Selvi began to give. She learned how to sew and started a tailoring shop to supplement her husband's small income. Instead of losing money at the market by being cheated she could now insist on the proper change. She carried herself with new dignity. She cleaned her house and insisted her children go to school. She would often say that she now had two great loves—the love of her Savior and of her husband.

The villagers wanted to know what changed Selvi, so she invited them to her house to join a prayer cell. As they prayed, Jesus came into them and Selvi encouraged them how to form prayer cells in their homes. In addition to her little prayer cell, four more prayer cells were formed and many rivers of life began to flow, transforming other families in the area. As the rivers of water flowed into the village, the entire village seemed to come to life—to new life in Jesus.

That living water is flowing in every nation on earth, bringing eternal life and forming new rivers. Someday when Jesus comes again the earth will be transformed and the old will pass away and new, eternal life will fill the earth.

Learn it:

1. How does this picture portray the life of a disciple of Jesus?
2. Why do we feel like "leaky old buckets" sometimes?
3. Did Paul feel like a leaky bucket according to 2 Corinthians 12:7–10? How did he get over those feelings?
4. In what ways did God use Selvi to bring life to her village?

Do it:

How is witnessing to others about Jesus like being a life-giver? How does the picture of rivers of water flowing from us make us want to witness?

Prayer: Dear Savior, grant that this day Your rivers of life may flow from us into our brothers and sisters, our parents, our uncles and aunts, and our children so that new rivers of living water may begin to flow. Grant that all around us we may see Your eternal life transforming families, villages, states, and entire nations. In Your name we pray. Amen.

* * * * *

Day Six: "Fruit Production"

"He who believes in Me, as the scripture says . . . from within him shall flow rivers of living water. *Now this He said about the Spirit, which those were to receive who believed in Him.*" John 7:38, 39

A monthly harvest: One of the most amazing things in Ezekiel's vision is the picture of the fruit trees. There are four things about these trees that are surprising.

- The first is that they bear very rich and abundant fruit on soil that never produced anything. God loves to transform selfish people into generous people! This is like making a fruit tree take root and grow in ground that never produced anything.

- The second is that their leaves don't wither. In other words the trees don't die. When Christ comes into us we start to live eternal life now! That life will not wither or die.
- A third thing is that not only do they bear fruit for food but their leaves are good for healing. Our purpose is both to strengthen others through teaching God's Word and also to bring healing to them.
- The final picture of these trees is the most amazing. Most of the trees we see bear fruit only once or twice a year, but the trees in Ezekiel's vision bear fruit every single month of the year. We are to bear continuous fruit through the rivers which flow through us and out of us.

John, the writer of the last book of the Bible, was very familiar with the trees in Ezekiel's vision. When God revealed heaven to John He described heaven as having trees like those pictured in Ezekiel. The water of life flows down from the throne of God in a "crystal river" through the middle of the street of the great city. On each side of the street, as in Ezekiel's vision, stand the trees bearing fruit every month. The leaves of the trees are for the healing of the nations (Revelation 22:1–2).

When the Spirit comes into us (as He did to His church on Pentecost [Acts 2] after Jesus ascended), He comes to enable us to bear fruit. The pictures of the trees are pictures of transformed Christians. Our function in fruit bearing is:

- To nourish and feed others spiritually.
- To bring healing to others.
- To show eternal life (leaves which do not wither) through our care and concern for others.
- To bear a continuous harvest of rich fruit.

The three marble players: Many years ago when I was reviewing a large Children's Bible Club program in Hyderabad, I saw three naughty-looking boys standing in the back row. You could see their eyes sparkle with mischief. I asked the director who they were. He told me they were marble players, skipping school day after day to gamble by playing marbles. He said that they were very bad, causing trouble at school and beating up their brothers and sisters and being disobedient to their parents.

But then Jesus came into their hearts during Children's Bible Club and they were transformed. They were filled with His Holy Spirit and the Holy Spirit began to grow the fruit of love in their lives. After several months they had become model students in school. They showed respect for their parents and love and consideration for their brothers and sisters. Fruit was growing! They stopped merely getting. They started to give and receive by returning their parents' love in concern for their brothers and sisters and by being obedient. *"But the fruit of the Spirit is love, joy, peace, patience, kindness, goodness, faithfulness, gentleness and self-control" (Galatians 5:22).*

The transformed son: In a daily Children's Development Club, we interviewed a mother who obviously was not a follower of Jesus but was letting her son come to the club each day. When we asked why she did that she said that he came in order to learn about Jesus so that he could teach the family about Jesus. She said that he had become so loving, so kind, so caring that they could not believe the wonderful changes. The young boy had become a temple in which Jesus lives. Rivers of living water were flowing out of him, transforming his family. Soon his parents and brothers and sisters would have Jesus living in them also and they in turn would become rivers of living water from which both life and fruit would come.

A new self-image: When Jesus comes into us He transforms us so that from us rivers, many rivers, of living water will flow out of us, bringing life and fruit where before there was only barrenness and deadness. This is who we are. We are not "no-bodies." We are not outcastes. We are children of the King of kings, the dwelling place of the Most High God. Jesus lives in us. Praise His name.

"I HAVE BEEN CRUCIFICIED WITH CHRIST AND I NO LONGER LIVE BUT CHRIST LIVES IN ME!"

May the light of Jesus shine from us and may the living waters flow out of us so that all people may live and bear the fruit of the Spirit!

Learn it:
What are the four characteristics of the fruit produced by the streams of living water?

Do it:
Give a practical example of each of the characteristics by describing a real or imaginary scene in your life.

Prayer: Precious Savior, how we praise You for the wonder of salvation. What a glorious gift You have given us. Fill us with Your presence. Make us know where You are and Who You are. And please, Lord Jesus, help us know that You are in us and that You are the King of kings and Lord of life. May we know what You want to do with us, namely, to make Your light shine through us and to have the rivers of living water flow from us. In Your name we pray, Amen.

* * * * *

Day Seven: Reflection

1. What did you like about this study this week?
2. How would you answer the question: "Who are you?" after have studied this material?
3. Was there anything that you did not like or did not understand?
4. What unique new lessons did you learn about God?
5. Did this lesson help you in any practical way. Explain how.

To order more copies of this book, "The New You," as well as additional books by Dr. John DeVries, contact Mission India as follows:

MISSION INDIA
PO Box 141312
Grand Rapids, MI 49514-1312
Phone: (616) 453-8855
Toll free: (877) 644-6342
Email: books@missionindia.org
Web: www.missionindia.org